Yucatecans in Dallas, Texas
Breaching the Border, Bridging the Distance

Rachel H. Adler
The College of New Jersey

PEARSON

Boston   New York   San Francisco
Mexico City   Montreal   Toronto   London   Madrid   Munich   Paris
Hong Kong   Singapore   Tokyo   Cape Town   Sydney

For my family

Series Editor: Jennifer Jacobson
Composition and Prepress Buyer: Linda Cox
Manufacturing Buyer: JoAnne Sweeney
Editorial-Production Coordinator: Mary Beth Finch
Editorial-Production Service: Omegatype Typography, Inc.
Electronic Composition: Omegatype Typography, Inc.

For related titles and support materials, visit our online catalog at www.ablongman.com.

Between the time Website information is gathered and then published, it is not unusual for some sites to have closed. Also, the transcription of URLs can result in typographical errors. The publishers would appreciate notification where these errors occur so that they may be corrected in subsequent editions.

ISBN: 0-205-34989-7

Printed in the United States of America

10   9   8   7   6   5   4   3   2   1   08   07   06   05   04   03

All photos © Rachel Adler.

Contents

Foreword to the Series

The United States is now experiencing the largest wave of immigration in the country's history. New immigrants from Asia, Latin America, and the Caribbean are changing the American ethnic landscape.

Until recently, immigration was associated in the minds of many Americans with the massive influx of southern and eastern Europeans at the turn of the twentieth century. Since the late 1960s, America has again become a country of large-scale immigration, this time attracting newcomers from developing societies of the world, the vast majority from Asia, Mexico, Central and South America, and the Caribbean. The number of foreign-born is at an all-time high: an estimated 28.4 million immigrants were living in the United States in 2000. Although immigrants are a smaller share of the nation's population than they were at the beginning of the twentieth century—10 percent in 2000 compared to 15 percent in 1910—recent immigrants are having an especially dramatic impact because their geographic concentration is so great. In 2000, six states—California, New York, Florida, Texas, New Jersey, and Illinois—accounted for 71 percent of the immigrant population. Los Angeles, New York, Miami, San Francisco, Chicago, Washington, D.C., and Houston are, increasingly, immigrant cities with new ethnic mixes. And it is not just America's major urban centers that are experiencing immigrant inflows. Many smaller cities and towns also have growing immigrant populations.

Who are the new immigrants? What are their lives like here? How are they redefining themselves and their cultures?

And how are they contributing to a new and changing America? The *New Immigrants* series provides a set of case studies that explores these themes among a variety of groups. The books in the series are written by recognized experts who have done extensive in-depth research on particular immigrant groups. The groups represent a broad range of today's arrivals, coming from a variety of countries and cultures. The studies, based on research done in different parts of the country, cover a wide geographical range, from New York to California.

Most of the books in the series are written by anthropologists, although several sociologists are represented as well. All draw on qualitative research that shows what it means to be an immigrant in America today. As part of each study, individual immigrants tell their stories, which will help give a sense of the experiences and problems of the newcomers. Through the case studies, a dynamic picture emerges of the way immigrants are carving out new lives for themselves at the same time as they are creating a new and more diverse America.

The ethnographic case study, long the anthropologist's trademark, provides a depth often lacking in research on immigrants in the United States. Moreover, many anthropologists, like a number of authors in the *New Immigrants* series, have done research in the country of origin as well as in the United States. Having field experience at both ends of the migration chain makes anthropologists particularly sensitive to the role of transnational ties that link immigrants to their home societies. With first-hand experience of immigrants in their home cultures, anthropologists are also well positioned to appreciate continuities as well as changes in the immigrant setting.

As immigrants become a growing presence in American society, it becomes more important than ever to learn about the newcomers and to hear their voices. The case studies in the *New Immigrants* series will help readers understand the cultures and lives of the newest Americans and bring out the complex ways that recent immigrants are coming to terms with and creatively adapting to life in a new land.

NANCY FONER
Series Editor

Acknowledgments

This work would not have been possible without the assistance of so many people. First and foremost, I owe an enormous debt of gratitude to all of the people of "Kaal," Yucatán. Thank you for sharing your knowledge, thank you for your gracious hospitality, and thank you for your sincere friendship. You have changed my life forever.

I would like to thank the Department of Anthropology, the Friends of Latin American Studies, and the Graduate Student Association of Arizona State University for granting financial support for this research. Thanks are also in order for Delta Publishing Company for sending ESL materials to use with the Yucatecos. I am grateful to Debbie Compte and the Office of Academic Affairs at the College of New Jersey (TCNJ), for the generous grant that paid for preparation of this manuscript. Thank you to the Department of Sociology and Anthropology at TCNJ for contributing funds for the presentation of some of this data at the 2001 American Anthropological Association meetings.

A warm thank you to Caroline Brettell, who so wisely suggested that I submit this manuscript to the *New Immigrants* series, and to the rest of my dissertation committee, Robert Alvarez and John Martin. I am indebted to my mentor, John Chance, whose wisdom, dedication, and kindness will always inspire me. Many other friends and colleagues contributed to this work by giving feedback, advice, and/or by supporting me in this endeavor and I appreciate their assistance: Carol Adler; David Adler; Grace Bascope; Sandra Bever; Anthony Call; Leo Chavez; Tim Clydesdale; Armin

Ek Yeh; Anne Goldberg; Michael Kearney; Ian Mast; Michelle Moran-Taylor; Stephen Perkins; Eugenia Shanklin; Tamar Diana Wilson; and Paul Zoltan. I am especially grateful to Nancy Foner for her spectacular job editing this book. I would be remiss if I failed to mention Carol and David Adler's meticulous copyediting of this manuscript. Of course, all shortcomings are mine alone. Finally, I would like to thank my entire extended family for their constant and loyal support and confidence in me.

Introduction

This is a study of a group of people who migrate between a particular town in Northern Yucatán, Mexico, and a neighborhood in Dallas, Texas. Like so many other migrants in the United States today, the migrants from Yucatán do not arrive in Dallas and cut social ties to their hometown. Rather, they maintain strong community and kinship affiliation to their fellow townsmen, both migrant and non-migrant. The maintenance of social fields across political borders is called *transnational migration,* and this book contributes to a burgeoning literature in anthropology that shows how the local and global are interconnected and fundamentally inseparable (Appadurai 1991, 1996a, 1996b; Basch, Glick-Schiller, and Szanton-Blanc 1994; Guarnizo and Smith 1999; Hannerz 1996; Kearney 1995; Smith 1999; among others). Transnational social connections are forged and maintained by migrants, many of whom have limited economic means and little access to institutional power in either of the two nation-states that they traverse.

Anthropological research captures the human dimension of migration and reveals how migration is actually lived by people (Brettell 2000:118). A number of recent writings view migration as a social process that develops patterns and structures of its own, and my study follows this approach (Alvarez 1991; Chávez 1998; Georges 1990; Goldring 1999; Grasmuck and Pessar 1991; Hagan 1994; among others). In this book I am careful to focus on the motivations, actions, and ideas of migrants themselves. In the pages that follow, case studies and ethnographic description are presented to illustrate the migration experience of the Yucatecans and to show that migrants, the "locals," are active participants in creating and transforming the "global." The organization of the contemporary world into nation-states and the domination of global capitalism certainly limit migrants' choices and influence their access to wealth, power, and prestige, but they do not determine migrants' actions. Migrants can act in opposition to, and circumvent institutions and social conventions that get in the way of their life projects. They can, in the course of pursuing their goals, create alternative social practices that may eventually become "normal" and accepted as part of the status quo (see Giddens 1979; 1984; 1995).

In order to capture human agency (as I define it, the ability of people to act outside of social conventions) and to understand the multifaceted nature of the migration experience, I have developed the term *migrant agendas*. Migrant agendas are complex sets of ideas and values that include the goals and motivations for migration, plans in migration, and the coordination of general life goals (life projects) with migration. These are in no way fixed or unchanging. Migrant agendas are modified as a result of changes in access to resources or in response to new circumstances. My purpose in focusing on migrant agendas is to emphasize agency in the migration process and show how migrants' actions can lead to social change. Even though I am only capturing an ethnographic snapshot of migrant agendas as I observed them in the course of my research, my study shows that migrant agendas are complex and diachronic (they change through time).

This book is also about transnationalism. The case of Yucatecans in Dallas fits Peggy Levitt's definition of a transnational village, in which many people from a relatively small and well-defined sending community migrate to a particular receiving area and maintain transnational ties (2001:213). In this formulation, the migrants' continued participation in their hometown transforms it to such an extent that non-migrants are also brought into the web of transnationalism (Ibid:11). This is brought about by social remittances—that is, ideas and practices that migrants bring with them on visits home that are noticed and then copied by non-migrants (Ibid:11). Migration itself becomes increasingly attractive to non-migrants as it becomes normative practice. The transnational social field is likely to persist because it becomes a general social pattern that can continue even if some individuals cease to participate in it. In the Yucatecan case, every year more and more people become migrants. The newcomers to Dallas keep transnationalism alive for the Yucatecan migrants. Thus, transnationalism does not just come "from above" in the form of global capital flows or multinational corporate interests. It also comes "from below" (Smith and Guarnizo 1999) because of the actions of migrants.

STUDYING YUCATECANS IN DALLAS

I first learned of a group of Yucatecans living in Dallas from a local photojournalist who specialized in documenting migrant communities in Dallas. The photographer told me that there were several hundred Yucatecans, all from the same town, living in a large apartment complex along one street within walking distance from my home. Excited about the possibility of "visiting Yucatán in Dallas," I asked for contact information. She told me about "Alfredo," a knowledgeable and gregarious man who had been in Dallas since 1969, and would later become (at least at the first stage of my research) my key informant.

I arrived at the apartment complex on a hot day in August 1997 with Alfredo's address in hand. The street had rows of apartments and I could not locate the address. I approached a group of Latino teenage boys in the parking lot, each of whom was wearing oversized pants and expensive-looking tennis shoes, and asked if they knew Alfredo. They did not know him by name but when I mentioned that he was Yucatecan they knew immediately where "the Yucatecos" lived and pointed me in the right direction. I knocked on Alfredo's door and was greeted warmly by him and his wife and son. Alfredo poured me a glass of fresh watermelon juice and began to tell me about the restaurant that he and his wife Luz operated from their apartment each weekend. He invited me to come and eat there so that I could meet some of the many Yucatecans who were all from "Kaal," a pseudonym for a town in Northern Yucatán.

Thus began my interaction with Yucatecans in Dallas, and my weekly visits to the apartment complex turned into daily visits as I began offering free English classes to anyone who was interested. As I became a familiar presence to more and more of the 200 or so Yucatecan migrants (including men, women, and children), I became known as "*la maestra*" (the teacher) and people began to call me and request lessons. My first class consisted of eight women friends, none of whom spoke more than a few words of English. We met twice a week in the evenings while their husbands were working at restaurant jobs. Our bi-weekly meetings were social events that always turned into gossip sessions by the end of class. This core group of women included me in many of their social plans and became my closest informants throughout the two years of my research.

I visited Kaal, Yucatán, for the first time just before the New Year's celebration in January 1998. I arrived in a taxi with Alfredo's mother's address in my pocket and the cab driver helped me find her house. As we reached the house he pointed out that it was a *casa buena* (good house) because it was made of concrete construction as opposed to the numerous adobe structures. I arrived eager to meet Alfredo's family, and they invited me to stay with them to celebrate New Year's Eve.

The following day, the women prepared food in the afternoon and at about nine o'clock in the evening the entire family sat in the main room of the house eating appetizers and drinking Bacardi with mixers. The door to the main room, which opened onto the plaza, remained open and visitors came in and out, sitting for a time and chatting. As midnight approached the excitement was palpable; when the hour struck, the many *viejos* (mannequins stuffed with fireworks and flammable material), propped against the outside walls of homes along the main street of the town, were set on fire as onlookers from all over the town stood and cheered. The burning of the *viejos* symbolizes the termination of the old year and the ushering in of a new, "young" year. We then sat down for a midnight meal and champagne and did not retire to our hammocks until about 5:00 a.m.

One day after the holiday I met with the mayor of the town in the government building located in the central plaza. Later, his wife gave me a guided tour of Kaal, taking me to visit families who had migrant kin in Dallas. I noticed that the families of the migrants had many electronic goods, such as VCRs, stereos, and television sets, undoubtedly purchased in the United States and brought by migrants. Framed posters of the Dallas skyline and Dallas Cowboys' team paraphernalia were common sights. People asked me about their migrant relatives and several gave me letters and gifts to take to them when I went back to Dallas.

When I returned to Dallas the following week, news spread quickly that I had been to Kaal. This definitely changed and improved my status in the eyes of the migrants. Once they knew that I had been to their hometown, people were eager to talk about their lives and families there. I became accepted by the community in Kaal and by the migrants in Dallas and I was regularly invited to birthday parties, baby showers, and weddings in both places. I was also asked to teach additional English classes, give advice about immigration issues, take people shopping and to other appointments, translate, and help several women find jobs. I tried to do as much as I could to help people in all of these endeavors, all the while communicating to them how much they were helping me with my research.

OVERVIEW

In the pages that follow, I present detailed case studies of the lives of Yucatecan migrants to illustrate their goals and life projects. Throughout the book, I use pseudonyms to protect informants' identities. I also use a pseudonym for the town in Yucatán. I begin, in Chapters 2 and 3, by discussing the context in which the United States–Yucatecan migration takes place. I provide a historical overview and description of the conditions that set the stage for out-migration from the town of Kaal, Yucatán, in the northern region of the Yucatecan peninsula. I also describe the setting in which migrants live in Dallas. Chapter 4 explores the implications of crossing borders for the lives of the Yucatecan migrants; Chapter 5 examines transnational migration, showing how the transnational social field that migrants create is a product of their migrant agendas. Chapter 6 looks at migration as a gendered process, comparing the migrant agendas of men and women. In the concluding chapter, I come back to some general issues about the way migrant agency is potentially transformative and can lead to new social practices and societal change.

2

Kaal as Context

With more than thirty languages spoken, Mexico is a diverse country with a complex and fascinating history. Mexico is part of *Mesoamerica,* the term used by anthropologists to refer to the area of Middle America with an indigenous heritage. After the conquest of Mexico by Spain in 1521, the indigenous peoples of Mexico endured three centuries of Spanish colonialism. After independence in 1821 there was a struggle between the creoles (the white descendants of the Spaniards), who wanted to preserve their wealth and power, and the mestizos (mixed descendants of Indians and Spaniards) and Indians, who wanted to improve their social status (Carmack et al. 1996:216–217). The period of liberal reforms began under the two terms of Benito Juárez (1854–1862, 1867–1872), a mestizo with Indian ancestry, and was crystallized under the dictatorship of Porfirio Díaz (1872–1910). During this period the hacienda was the primary means to achieve the ideals of capitalist economic development and modernization. The hacienda system, in which products such as coffee, bananas, cattle, and henequen were cultivated by wage laborers (or indebted peons) for export to the United States and Europe, expanded during the period of liberal reforms. The land used was often taken from peasants who depended upon it for subsistence. The negative social consequences of the liberal reforms and the hacienda system for peasants led to social upheaval in the form of the Mexican Revolution (1910–1917). In the post-revolutionary period a program of land redistribution was instituted whereby land was returned to peasant communities in the form of communal land grants called *ejidos*. In 1992, under the presidency of Salinas de Gortari, the ejido system was challenged by a revision of the constitution that allowed for the privatization of these lands. While some towns and villages in Mexico have sold off their ejidal lands, others have refused to do so.

There are several geographical and cultural regions in Mexico, each with a distinct history both before and after the Spanish conquest. The most basic division is between lowlands and highlands. The highlands are areas above 1,000 meters elevation, including the central plateau of Mexico, the mountainous areas of Oaxaca, and the intermontaine basin of Chiapas (Carmack et al. 1996:10–12). The soils in these areas are particularly fertile because of volcanic activity and the previous existence of lakes. Thus, agriculture has tended to be intensive in the highlands, and population centers have been dense. Lowland areas, on the other hand, are located along the Pacific, Gulf of Mexico, and Caribbean coasts. The soils in the lowlands are less fertile than in the highlands and agriculture has been more extensive. The population is more widely scattered and urbanization has not been as widespread as in higher altitudes (Carmack et al. 1996:11). The Yucatán peninsula is in the lowlands.

Although many people speak indigenous languages in Mexico, considerable cultural and social mixing—called *meztizaje* (blending) has occurred—between people of indigenous and European ancestries. In some regions of Mexico, there are high concentrations of people who speak indigenous languages and identify themselves as members of indigenous communities. Rural areas of Oaxaca, Chiapas, and Yucatán are such places. Urban areas and some central and western states (Michoacán, Guanajuato, Jalisco, Sinaloa) and northern states (Sonora, Chihuahua, Coahuila) generally have lower concentrations of indigenous speakers, although many indigenous speakers do migrate to cites and retain their languages.

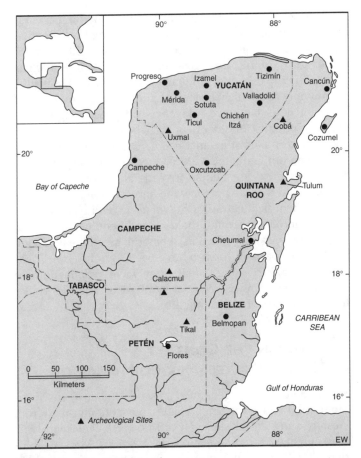

MAP 2.1 Yucatan Peninsula

Source: From Agrarian Reform and Public Enterprise in Mexico: The Political Economy of Yucatan's Henequen Industry, by Jeffery Brannon and Eric N. Baklanoff. Copyright 1987 by University of Alabama Press. Reprinted by permission.

Yucatán is one of three states on the Yucatán peninsula (see Map 2.1). The entire peninsula is characterized by the predominance of a Yucatec Mayan ethnic identity, culture, and history. In Mexico, people tend to deny their knowledge of an indigenous language, especially when they are among those who are not native speakers. Unfortunately, in most of

Mexico there is a social stigma attached to anything considered indigenous (except ancient ruins and anything else that attracts the tourists' gaze—see Bonfil Batalla 1996; Friedlander 1975). In Yucatán, however, Yucatec Maya is a *lingua franca;* it is the principal language spoken on the peninsula, second only to Spanish. Instead of hiding their knowledge of an indigenous language, Mayan is often the language of choice, especially for older people. To be sure, discrimination and prejudice persist against people considered indigenous in Yucatán but, among Yucatecos themselves, there is also a sense of ethnic pride. People are generally proud to be from Yucatán, and they do not view the outward symbols of Mayanness such as the traditional *huipil* (a white dress with bright embroidery around the neck and hemline) and *rebozo* (shawl), or speaking Maya as shameful, as indigenous people in other parts of Mexico have been found to do (Friedlander 1975). To some extent, they have redefined these items and customs as regional symbols of Yucatán, rather than as markers of Indian identity.

YUCATÁN IN THE CONTEXT OF UNITED STATES–MEXICO MIGRATION

Social scientists have generated a wealth of data about Mexican immigrants in the United States, most on migration from Western and Central Mexico (Cardoso 1980; Dinerman 1982; Massey, Alarcón, Durand, and González 1987; Massey, Goldring, and Durand 1994; Mines 1981; Mines and Anzaldua 1982; Rouse 1991; Smith 1993) and from Oaxaca (Grimes 1998; Kearney 2000; Nagengast and Kearney 1990; Nagengast, Stavenhagen, and Kearney 1992; Rivera Salgado 1999). Also, there has been considerable research on Maya populations from Guatemala (Burns 1993; Hagan 1994; Loucky 1992; Repak 1995). Yucatecans are an interesting case because they are Mayan but they are also Mexicans. Also noteworthy is that few of them live in the United States. What has kept them from going there? It is not that they are from the "Indian" culture region. After all, most Oaxacans and many Guatemalans are also indigenous. It can't be merely geographical distance; neither Oaxaca nor Guatemala is any closer to the United States than the Yucatán. In fact, by airplane, Yucatán is about the same distance or closer to some parts of the United States than Michoacán and Guanajuato, the two states that have historically sent the most migrants northward. How can we account for the relative paucity of Yucatecan migrants in the United States in 2002? Answering this question requires an analysis of regional Yucatecan history. Three main factors are involved: the development and proliferation of the henequen economy in the 19th and early 20th centuries; the nature of the Mexican railroad infrastructure in the late 19th and early 20th centuries; and the development of Cancún as a tourist town in the 1970s.

Henequen in Yucatán

The remarkable success of the henequen industry in the northwest portion of the state of Yucatán deferred Yucatecan migration to the United States. Henequen, also known as sisal, is a fibrous plant that is used to make rope. Beginning in the mid-19th century and extending to the early 20th century, this rope was in high demand because it was used for binder twine in U.S. agriculture. The henequen zone includes the capital city of Mérida and surrounding towns and villages—where Kaal is located. In this region, the rocky soil is suitable for this slow-growing, fibrous agave plant. Although some henequen was grown during the colonial period, it was not until after Mexican independence that that the crop was systematically cultivated for export (Wells 1985:21). By 1847, henequen had become the second leading export from the region; the leading export was sugar (Ibid:21–22).

In the early to mid-19th century, henequen and sugar plantations expanded. Although henequen production is labor intensive, it used land around Mérida that was already part of the hacienda system (Ibid:30). Sugar production, however, required the acquisition of new land. *Hacendados* (hacienda owners) aggressively took over frontier land for their sugar operations and the native populations resisted appropriation of the land that they needed for their extensive *milpa* (corn) production (Ibid:30). In 1847, these "frontier" (unsettled) Maya fought back against the white hacendados, initiating the peasant revolt known as the Caste War. This conflict did not end until 1852.

The Caste War had drastic political and economic consequences for Yucatán. What is now the state of Campeche, for example, seceded in 1858 and took with it more than a third of the state's former territory (Ibid:31). The sugar industry was effectively destroyed because most of the fighting took place in the southeastern part of the peninsula, where the industry was located. The cattle industry was also adversely affected as soldiers slaughtered cattle by the thousands in order to feed themselves during the war (Ibid:31). The henequen zone near Mérida, however, remained intact, and the production of henequen was sharply increased in 1860. Among the reasons was the rising demand for the product in the United States (Wells 1985:29), and that Yucatán had favorable growing conditions and was close to the United States, whose rapidly expanding agricultural sector was becoming increasingly dependent on henequen (Brannon and Baklanoff 1987:33). U.S. demand for henequen intensified when, in 1878, Cyrus McCormick invented the twine-binding reaper, which necessitated the use of henequen and further increased demand. After 1880, the United States consumed ninety percent of Yucatán's henequen (Brannon and Baklanoff 1987: 38). By the turn of the century the entire Yucatecan economy was geared towards monocrop production and export of henequen (Wells 1985:29–30).

The striking success of the henequen enterprise combined with the history of detachment from the rest of Mexico led Yucatán's social structure to evolve differently than in other regions of Mexico. (Yucatán was actually independent from Mexico between 1839 and 1846.) The legacy of henequen was a plantation society with a class structure that had more in common with the sugar societies of the Caribbean than other regions of Mexico (Wells 1985:184). One of the most striking facts about the 1880–1915 period in Yucatán is how so few families controlled so much land, political power, and productive capacity (1982:37). A small, close-knit group of about twenty to thirty families controlled 80 to

90 percent of the henequen in Yucatán. This tiny oligarchy came to be called the *casta divina* (the divine caste). The rural peons, who in Gilbert Joseph's account were literally slaves, constituted the overwhelming majority of the population (1982:37). The polarized class structure of rich and poor meant that there was no middle class to challenge the hegemony of the *casta divina*. Thus, especially in its early years, the Mexican Revolution was a relatively peaceful time in Yucatán in comparison to the violent bloodshed that occurred in the rest of Mexico. The social relations of production of henequen were brutal for peasants in Yucatán, but the oligarchy was so firmly entrenched that Mayan workers felt powerless to do anything about it. The Revolution was largely ignored, as Yucatán was busy producing henequen for the world market (Wells 1985:183–185). Thus, as rural peoples in other parts of Mexico were fleeing to the United States to avoid violence and to search for employment, Yucatecans stayed in Yucatán. The geographical and cultural isolation of Yucatán was exacerbated by the remarkable success of the henequen trade.

Railroads in Mexico

The isolation of Yucatán was further reinforced by the nature of the railroad infrastructure. The railroads played a crucial role in facilitating the migration of Mexicans—from other regions of Mexico—to the United States in the late 19th and early 20th centuries. Railroad construction and maintenance was one of the first sources of employment for Mexican migrants from central and western Mexico, and from there they moved into other industries such as steel and meatpacking (Massey et al. 1987:41–42). Mexican migrants also ended up settling in the places in the United States that were railroad hubs such as Los Angeles, San Antonio, El Paso, and Chicago. Map 2.2 shows the pattern of the railroads in the United States by 1900. By the time of the Mexican Revolution in 1910, migration to the United States was well established, with 18,000 immigrants per year. By the 1920s that number increased to 49,000 immigrants per year (Ibid:42). Yet the railroad lines in Mexico did not reach Yucatán, as Map 2.3

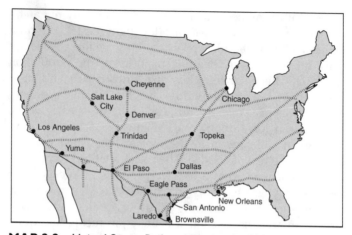

MAP 2.2 United States Railroad Pattern by 1900

Source: From Mexican Emigration to the United States 1897–1931, *by Lawrence Cardoso. Copyright © 1980, The Arizona Board of Regents. Reprinted by permission of the University of Arizona Press.*

clearly shows. Most immigrants to the U.S. came from western and central Mexico (especially Jalisco, Michoacán, Guanajuato, and Zacatecas), areas where railroad lines were connected to the north. Indeed, even in the 1940s, well-known anthropologist Robert Redfield commented that "in everything but literal truth [Yucatán] is an island…inaccessible except by boat or airplane (Redfield 1941, cited in Brannon and Baklanoff 1987:20)." Geographically, the peninsula was isolated in that an area of dense jungle and swamps separated it from Chiapas. As a result, railroad and highway links between Mérida and central Mexico did not exist until the early 1960s. Until then, the ports in Yucatán were the main link between the peninsula and the rest of the world (Brannon and Baklanoff 1987:20).

Henequen entrepreneurs promoted railroad construction, at first as a means of incorporating the marginalized southeastern part of the peninsula into the Northwest henequen zone (Wells 1985:90). Since the henequen elite developed the railroad infrastructure, it was built to facilitate the henequen trade. Mérida was the hub of the railroad system and it was

MAP 2.3 Mexican Railroads by 1910 with Connections to United States Lines

Source: From Mexican Emigration to the United States 1897–1931, by Lawrence Cardoso. Copyright © 1980, The Arizona Board of Regents. Reprinted by permission of the University of Arizona Press.

connected to outlying henequen-producing towns and villages. In the span of twenty-five years (1874–1899) the entire henequen zone had a system of railroad tracks and tramways, all leading to Mérida and to the port of Progreso (Ibid:92). Ultimately, the southeast was completely left out of this development. By 1890, Yucatán had one of the most extensive rail systems of any state in Mexico (Brannon and

Baklanoff 1987:38). But the railroad infrastructure was completely internal; it was not connected to the rest of Mexico. This helps to account for the absence of Yucatecans in the United States at the turn of the twentieth century. The railroad infrastructure was only connected with the rest of Mexico in the 1960s, around the time that Cancún became developed as a tourist zone.

Cancún: The Development of a Tourist Mecca

A third explanation for the low level of Yucatecan migration to the United States is Yucatán's proximity to Cancún. The popularity of Cancún as a travel destination has been a magnet for internal migration. The first hotel in Cancún was completed in 1974. By 1987, Cancún was receiving 1,000,000 tourists per year who were spending about four million dollars per day (Re Cruz 1996:144, 146). Today Cancún is one of the most popular tourist destinations for vacationing Americans, especially college students.

Cancún was planned in the late 1960s and constructed in the 1970s. According to a recent travel guide:

Unlike Acapulco or Puerto Vallarta, which were idyllic little villages until tourism replaced fishing as the major source of income, Cancún is a made-to-order resort, built specifically for tourism where the wild jungle met a deserted shore. One creation story claims that around 1968 a computer program churned out the Cancún location after being fed vital statistics from all over Mexico. The statistical parameters included climate, beach conditions and proximity to the United States. Whether the legend is true or not, we know that before the bankers and government officials realized that Cancún's reliable sunshine, warm weather and sparkling waters provided the perfect place to build a new world-class seaside resort, nothing much was here. Just some small ruins of the ancient Maya civilization out on the barren dunes and in what is now the ferry and fishing town of Puerto Juarez, and scrub brush (Conord and Conord 1998:89–90).

The construction of a mega-resort from scratch demanded labor. Migrants from towns and villages throughout the peninsula sent migrants to work in construction. Many of the Kaaleños in Dallas worked in Cancún in the 1970s and 1980s. Today, many men and women from Kaal live and/or work in Cancún. The service sector provides many jobs for migrants willing to work in hotels and restaurants or as domestic servants. Anthropologist Sandra Bever (2000), who had originally wanted to do a comparative study of two Yucatecan villages, one with migration and one without, was unable to find a village that did not send migrants to Cancún! In general, many Yucatecan men who would have gone to the United States (or Mexico City) have gone to Cancún instead.

Network Migration and the Relative Paucity of Yucatecans in the United States

The history of henequen, railroads, and tourist development all have limited U.S.-bound migration from Yucatán. How does this fit in with perspectives that emphasize the network aspects of migration? United States–Mexico migration evolves similarly in Mexican rural communities (Durand and Massey 1992). That is, migration proceeds in stages (Massey, Goldring, and Durand 1994). In the earliest stages, few adults out-migrate to the United States. Most migrants are men, and their geographical destinations and occupational choices in the United States are limited. As migration progresses, it becomes a more generalized trend and women begin to migrate too. Concurrently, migrants begin to diversify both occupationally and residentially; no longer limited to a few types of jobs or to a particular geographical area in the U.S. (Massey, Goldring, and Durand 1994:1528–1529).

One recent study concludes that, "each act of migration itself creates the social structure needed to sustain it" (Massey et al. 1993:449). Although migration can begin with a single individual, it becomes a social process as relatives and friends follow. Tamar Diana Wilson calls this "network-mediated migration" (Wilson 1993:108). Yet, owing to the regional particulars of the Yucatecan political economy, Yucatán, unlike other regions of Mexico, is only at an early stage of the migration process. There is no long history of U.S.-bound migration from Yucatán because the henequen industry further isolated the already geographically remote region from the rest of Mexico. The railroad infrastructure reinforced this isolation until the 1960s. Soon after, the development of Cancún as a tourist location provided alternative means of employment, also deferring migration to the United States. In contrast, other regions of Mexico, which have been sending migrants to the United States since the 19th century, have developed broad and strong networks that have increased the rate of migration over time. The migration between Kaal, Yucatán, and Dallas, Texas, is new; although the first migrant arrived in Dallas in 1969, the chain migration did not really intensify until the early 1990s. Now that some Yucatecans live in the United States we should expect that their numbers will increase as social networks become more established. We can also expect that more women will migrate from Yucatán, and that they will go to places besides Dallas and the San Bernardino valley of California (the other receiving area for Kaaleños). It is likely that in a decade or so there will be substantial numbers of Yucatecans in the United States. It will be fascinating to trace the development of this relatively new migrant population to see how it compares with longstanding Mexican migrant communities.

LIVING IN KAAL

Kaal is a picturesque Yucatecan town and its layout is typical of Yucatecan towns. As of 1995 the population of the *municipio* (county) of Kaal was 5,621 and of the town itself, 4,869 (INEGI 1996). The beautiful colonial-era church (built in 1621) and the new government palace are in the center of town, forming a square that residents call the *plaza* or the *parque*. This central plaza is a community center with shady trees and places to sit and visit with neighbors. Around the *plaza* are stores and small businesses such as *tortillerías* and the small but modern marketplace. Those who live in houses built around the plaza are considered to be of higher social status than those living further away from the town's center. Homes near the plaza, like those in the city of Mérida, are made of brick and mortar construction with doors and windows that face onto the plaza. Other homes in Kaal are different. Traditional houses of adobe and thatched roof exist side by side with adobe houses with roofs of sheet metal and brick and mortar homes with thatched roofs. The quality of houses in Kaal varies; the condition of a house's construction is a good indicator of the residents' socioeconomic status. People build their homes over time; often a house comes to an abrupt end, and is open where it backs right into the *solar* (yard). Homeowners construct one main room first and then add a kitchen, separate bedrooms, and a bathroom. Adobe homes lack indoor plumbing, and people relieve themselves outside in an area behind the homesite area. A good number of brick and mortar homes have bathrooms, which are considered a luxury by many in the community. Very few people have hot water in their homes. In order to bathe comfortably during the rare months when the temperature in Yucatán cools down, water is heated up on a stove.

Most people in Kaal sleep in hammocks, which are hung onto metal hooks built into the walls of homes. Any room is a place where people can potentially sleep, and families tend to sleep together in one main room. Some families own beds but few actually sleep in them. Most prefer the cooling effect of a swinging hammock to a hot and uncomfortable bed.

Outside of the town's limits but still part of the municipio of Kaal are several outlying rural areas (*ranchos*) and former haciendas where people live in impoverished conditions. In these areas indoor plumbing is rare and only recently has there been electricity. Most people in these outlying areas are Maya speaking. In one hacienda, 293 out of 673 residents are monolingual Maya speakers; in the other areas Maya speakers are bilingual (INEGI 1996:612). Many residents of outlying areas own bicycles and travel into the center of Kaal to make purchases, attend religious fiestas, and go to the market. Some people who live in the town of Kaal consider residents of these outlying provinces to be backward and ignorant and there is much prejudice and discrimination against them.

Economy of Kaal

The primary economic activity in Kaal is henequen production. Most non-migrant men work at harvesting and cutting henequen, some of which is processed into sisal using the defibrillating machine located on the only former hacienda that has equipment still in operation. Others transport the unprocessed henequen to Mérida where they sell it directly to companies that process and sell it on the world market. Up until the 1990s, henequen production was principally ejidal; people participated and shared the profits communally. Under post-revolutionary land reform, many Yucatán haciendas were deemed ejidal lands. *Campesinos* (peasant farmers) continued to grow henequen under the ejidal system, in theory each farmer contributing labor to the production process and dividing the earnings according to how much labor each participant put in. After the Mexican government amended Article 27 of the Mexican constitution in 1994, ejidal lands could be privatized, and many former ejidal holdings in Yucatán are now privately owned. *Campesinos* working on former ejidal lands continue to produce the fibrous plant but they no longer are paid by the ejidal group. Now independent henequen farmers are responsible for all parts of the production process and their earnings come from selling henequen directly. People supplement henequen income by farming *milpa* and consuming at least some of what they produce. There are several privately owned ranches that employ people to take care of livestock, which includes both cattle and swine. Some residents have set up small stores in their homes where they supply neighbors with soda, canned goods, toilet paper, and other basic necessities. Quite a few women own sewing machines and make *huipiles* and urban style clothing to order. Others bake cakes for birthdays, weddings, and other occasions. Women who have been trained as beauty stylists cut and style hair in their homes. There are several *cantinas* (bars), owned by local families, where men spend their afternoons drinking and socializing. Near the center of town there are stores and a market where a number of women operate *loncherías* (market food stands), serving the regional food of Yucatán such as *tacos* (meat in a soft tortilla), *salbutes* (fried tortillas topped with meat and vegetables) and *panuchos* (tortillas filled with fried beans and topped with meat and vegetables).

Yet besides henequen production and *milpa* farming, several government jobs, small scale commerce, a few domestic positions for women, construction, and the kinds of activities just described, there is not sufficient economic opportunity in Kaal to meet subsistence needs. For this reason, many men and some unmarried women find it necessary to travel to Mérida in order to secure wage labor. Men most often work in the construction industry and women work as domestics. The fare for traveling to Mérida is currently seven pesos, and the expensive round trip often forces people to remain in Mérida for the entire week, returning home on Sunday to visit with family. Those who remain in Mérida during the week either stay with relatives or at their house of employment (in the case of domestics), or camp out at the construction site where they are employed.

Many men opt to migrate further away for work, returning home less frequently. Cancún is a popular place for Kaaleños and is a four-hour bus ride from Kaal. In the early to mid-1970s, when Cancún was targeted as a tourist development site by the Mexican government, men from Kaal migrated there to participate in the booming construction industry. Now, besides construction, men also work in the hotel and restaurant industries. Most of these men learned the restaurant trade in Dallas and, upon return to Yucatán, began to work in Cancún. Men often stay in Cancún for two weeks to a month and then return home for a short visit with their families.

Other men, frustrated with the low wages in Mexico, opt to go to the United States for work. The first Kaaleño to go to Dallas migrated there in 1969. He journeyed with friends from another town but was the pioneer migrant from Kaal. Once he was established in Dallas, he returned to Kaal and encouraged others to join him, hence the start of chain migration from Kaal to Dallas. Before this Texas-bound migration, several men had participated in the Bracero program in the post–World War II era, working as agricultural laborers in California. Another man, who claims that his father was the first person to go to the United States from Kaal, explained that his father's work as a bracero laborer funded the successful tortilla-making business that the family still runs to this day. The father sent money back to Kaal, and his sons bought the machinery necessary to begin producing tortillas for sale. Now they have several stores and are one of the wealthier families in Kaal. Today Dallas and the San Bernardino valley of California are the two principal U.S. receiving areas for migrants from Kaal, each with several hundred people from the town. There is a constant flow back and forth between Kaal and both areas.

In the 1990s, a maquiladora that produces clothing was established in a nearby town. This has created some jobs for people in Kaal. As in the maquiladoras along the U.S.-Mexican border, women constitute the majority of the workforce in these Yucatecan factories (Labrecque 1998:239). Yet it must be made clear that despite this kind of development, there is a paucity of economic opportunities in Kaal and this is the reason that people must go elsewhere to find employment.

Schools in Kaal

Kaal has two elementary schools, one junior high school (*secundaria*), and one high school (*preparatoria*). Attending junior high school and especially high school is considered a luxury. After junior high school some young women study in Mérida to be secretaries, seamstresses, or hairdressers. Young men and women who pass the qualification standards may go on to the teachers' college (*normal*) in the town of Chetumal. Some go to high school in Mérida because they consider the education there to be of higher quality.

Most of the migrants in Dallas did not attend school beyond *secundaria*. The reason is simple: their parents did not have enough money to allow them to continue their studies. By the time a young man in Kaal is fourteen or fifteen he is ready to begin working on his own in construction or other wage labor and is often encouraged by his family to do so. At this age young women can increase the amount of work they do in the household or begin working as domestics in Kaal or Mérida. School cuts down significantly on the amount of time that can be dedicated to working. Some men I spoke with explained that they quit school out of sheer exhaustion. Many worked with their fathers in the fields from four or five in the morning until noon. They returned home to eat and bathe and attended school in the afternoon. Evenings were spent doing homework in preparation for school the next day. For these men, school was not worth the economic or physical sacrifice. Most women cited economic reasons for not continuing their studies. Also, education for women is not as highly valued as it is for men; some women cited lack of parental encouragement and/or personal motivation as reasons for quitting school.

Religious Life in Kaal

The majority of residents of Kaal are Catholic although there are Protestant groups there as well. The Catholic ritual cycle dominates, and the town's calendar is organized around it. The most important fiesta is in September when the patron saint of the town, San Miguel Arcangel, is venerated. In May there is a fiesta for the image of the Virgin Mary. Both fiestas are celebrated with great fanfare. There is a celebration of the commencement of the fiesta, called the *vaquería*, on the first night of each fiesta, in which people gather on the plaza wearing their finest traditional Yucatecan clothing and dance the *jarana*, the official dance of Yucatán. Each night there is a dance in the plaza punctuated by fireworks, and carnival games and rides are set up for children's enjoyment. A bullring is constructed anew each year and people attend the bullfights hoping for some drama in the form of bloodshed.

July and August are the months for the celebration of *gremios*, which are parish associations dedicated to the veneration of the saints. Also in the summer there is a fiesta for the image of Christ that resides in the church. This fiesta is not as secularized as the other two and there are no bullfights or dances to celebrate it. Rather, there are daily processions, masses, and feasting.

An annual fiesta in Kaal venerates this image of the Virgin Mary.

On November 1 people celebrate the Day of the Dead by setting up shrines in their homes and placing the favorite food of their deceased loved ones upon it. Many go with flowers to the cemetery, where they sit and pray and symbolically visit with those who are no longer with them.

December 12 is the day of the Virgin of Guadalupe, celebrated with *promesas* (offerings) made to the virgin. On December 16 the *posadas* begin, when groups of people go from house to house, serenading the residents. Each evening the groups visit a different house, and they are invited in by the residents for refreshments. This symbolizes the Virgin Mary's search for a place to stay when she was pregnant with Jesus—and the *posadas* culminate on December 24 with the anniversary of his birth. On that day straws are drawn and a family is chosen to sponsor the *niño diós* (Son of God). The Jesus child is placed in someone's home each year on January 6, the Day of Kings. This is both an honor and a burden because it is expensive to feed all of the guests who come to visit throughout the year. The Day of Kings is the last celebration of Christmas.

Immediately before the Easter season, *carnaval* is celebrated by evening masquerade dances and heavy drinking. These end with Ash Wednesday, which represents the onset of the Easter season, a time of sacrifice, reflection, and seriousness. After Easter, those who can afford to do so celebrate the end of these solemn days by going to the beach for diversion. Once Holy Week ends, the May fiesta nears and the yearly cycle proceeds.

Throughout the year there are baptisms, *quinceañeras* (fifteenth birthday celebrations), first communions, and weddings, all of which involve religious ceremonies. A system of ritual kinship called *compadrazgo* regulates most of these celebrations, especially baptisms. Under the *compadrazgo* system a person is asked to "sponsor" the event. This sponsorship is a financial and religious obligation, which establishes a bond of ritual kinship between the sponsors (usually a married couple) and the parents of the celebrant. After the event, the two couples will refer to each other as *compadres*. In the case of baptism, the sponsors will be the godparents (*padrinos*) of the child. *Compadrazgo* sets the stage for a lifetime of reciprocity between the *compadres*. These reciprocal ties are frequently called upon in the migration experience.

Those few who are not Catholic do not participate in the religious parts of these rituals. Many Protestants do not drink alcohol or dance because of their religious convictions, which makes it impossible for them to even participate in the secularized activities such as dances. There is tension between Catholics and non-Catholics in the town, but most of the migrants in Dallas are Catholic.

The Catholic religious cycle is closely related to the pattern of migration to and from Kaal. Before every fiesta a number of migrants return to the town to visit. The days after a fiesta are the most popular times for new migrants to attempt to go to the United States for the first time. Since visiting migrants usually return to Dallas immediately following a fiesta or other religious holiday, they are often accompanied by a number of neophyte migrants who are making the trip for the first time.

THE MEANING OF "MAYANNESS"

Some scholars have no qualms about linking the modern Maya to their classic and post-classic Maya ancestors (Friedl, Schele, and Parker 1993; Kintz 1990). Other anthropologists disagree, citing the dramatic changes wrought by the colonial encounter in all of its stages, Independence, the Caste War, and the *Porfiriato* (the dictatorship of Porfirio Díaz) preceding the Mexican Revolution. Any vestiges of the ancient Maya have been so thoroughly transformed by all of these historical events, say these scholars, that the suggestion that the Maya of today are culturally the same as the Maya of pre-Hispanic contact is overstated (see Castañeda 1996; Farriss 1984; Haenn n.d.; Hervik 1999). The migrants from Kaal themselves acknowledge some distant connection with the pre-Hispanic past but they emphasize the transformations that occurred under colonialism and afterwards.

Indeed, Yucatán is a place where the classic Mayan civilization flourished, and evidence of this in the form of ruins and artifacts is almost everywhere. In Kaal there are unexcavated mounds, and the town's *cenote* (underground sinkhole) contains carvings etched in stone perhaps centuries ago. Nearby are the famous ruins of Chichén Itzá and to the south are the equally impressive remains of Uxmal. Upon visiting the capital city of Mérida, it is immediately apparent that tourists in Yucatán are there to see the ruins and to glance at the people who are touted to be the direct descendants of the classic Maya. According to some critical scholars, this romanticized image of the "modern Maya" and the

The monumental Mayan ruins of Chichén Itzá are about an hour away from the town of Kaal.

simplistic version of history upon which it rests are encouraged by various interests that profit from it, including the Mexican and international tourist industries, media publications such as *National Geographic* magazine, and even some scholarship (Castañeda 1996; Haenn n.d.; Hervik 1999). To some extent, people in Kaal have accepted this romanticization of the Mayan past and they certainly understand that most foreigners visit Yucatán to see ruins. When I arrived in the town ready to interview people and learn about local practices and culture, people offered to take me to Chichen Itzá or began to lecture me about ancient Mayan history. Many could not understand why I would be interested in their daily lives when there were so many important ruins of a *real* civilization in such close proximity. Yet people in Kaal do not describe themselves as direct descendants of the classic Maya. They insist that they are a mixture of Spanish and Maya and that the Maya that is spoken in Kaal is not *la verdadera Maya* (the real Maya) because it has Spanish words mixed in and is not *pura* (pure). Kaaleños consider all native Yucatecans to be part of a common cultural system.

Outsiders are called *huach* (in the case of Mexicans) and *gringos* (in the cases of North Americans and Europeans). Kaaleños consider themselves *mestizo* but they do not mean the same thing by this term that Mexicans from other parts of Mexico do. *Mestizo*, in other parts of Mexico, implies indigenous admixture but essentially means "non-Indian" in terms of culture. *Mestizo* in Yucatán also implies racial mixture but it implies Mayanness in the form of language, dress, and other cultural practices as well. But the term Maya can have negative overtones similar to the derogatory term *indio* (as noted by Friedlander 1975). Kaaleños, when asked where they are from by non-Yucatecans, often respond that they are from Mérida as a way to obscure the fact that they are from a Mayan-speaking town, which, especially to non-Yucatecan Mexicans, implies a poor, low-status background.

CONCLUSION

Kaal, Yucatán, is a typical town in Northern Yucatán. Most people make their living cultivating henequen and *milpa* and life revolves around the agricultural and ritual cycles. The community is mostly Catholic and the ceremonies venerating the saints are meaningful, community-defining events. What happens to Kaaleños when they reach Dallas? What are their lives like there? These are important questions that will be answered in the following chapter.

3

Yucatecans in the "Big D"

The Dallas Metroplex includes the city of Dallas ("the Big D") and the suburbs directly surrounding it. According to the 2000 census, 1,188,580 people live in the city of Dallas and 5,221,801 live in the entire Dallas–Fort Worth Metroplex. Like other Southwestern cities, Dallas has intense urban sprawl; it is challenging to get from one place to another without a car, and the heavy automobile use has caused a pollution crisis. There is a public transportation system, but it is inadequate and frustrates the many poor and working-class people who rely on it on a daily basis.

Like so many other U.S. cities, Dallas has witnessed a shift from a manufacturing-based to a service economy (Dallas Chamber of Commerce 1996:4; Sassen 1991; 2000). Services and wholesale/retail trade make up more than one half of the Dallas economy. Dallas is one of the most popular convention cities in the nation, and hosts about 3,000 conventions each year (Dallas Chamber of Commerce 2000:19). As an "international gateway" for business (Dallas Chamber of Commerce 1999) Dallas also has 28 consulates, 12 foreign trade offices, and 11 foreign banks. Indeed, total trade in the Dallas–Fort Worth Customs District has grown at a rate faster than in the nation. Dallas has 11 free trade zones where companies can avoid or defer U.S. customs duties, eight domestic financial institutions with international departments, and over 20 foreign-owned firms. In short, Dallas has many domestic firms that operate in global markets and/or that service foreign firms located in the city, epitomizing Saskia Sassen's idea of the "new urban economy" (Sassen 2000).

A good adjective to describe Dallas is "glitzy." The modern skyline is an architectural marvel that symbolizes the enormous wealth generated by the economic activities (banking, finance, and other high-level services) that go on inside the tall skyscrapers. There is a culture of conspicuous consumption on the part of the new wealthy in Dallas that might be considered gauche in other regions of the country. Besides buying and displaying expensive cars, palatial homes, and designer fashions, many wealthy Dallasites take part in a public social scene that rivals that in Hollywood. Much of this party-making takes place in expensive Dallas restaurants, owned and operated by celebrity chefs. Wealthy people in Dallas may desire to live a socially insulated life, but they inevitably come into contact with the poor and working classes. Poor people—mostly Mexican immigrants—are the ones who bus the tables, fill the water glasses, cook the meals, mow the lawns, clean the homes, and take care of the children of the wealthy in Dallas.

The city of Dallas has distinct neighborhoods that are, for the most part, residentially segregated along lines of social class, ethnicity, and race. The southern part of Dallas, which includes the downtown area, is predominantly African-American and Latino. To the east of the downtown is a Latino neighborhood, which has recently become heavily Asian, with among others, Vietnamese, Taiwanese, Korean, and Cambodian migrants. To the immediate west of the downtown there is another heavy concentration of Latinos and African-Americans. In the north are the predominantly White neighborhoods and Dallas' wealthiest areas. Not far from these upper and upper middle class White neighborhoods is "Brookhaven," a pseudonym for the area where almost all of the Yucatecans from Kaal live.

RACIAL AND ETHNIC RELATIONS IN DALLAS

Dallas is a diverse place, despite the racially based residential segregation that divides the Metroplex. This racial segregation is no doubt related to the apartheid conditions that the city's African-American residents had to endure after the

Civil War (Dulaney 1993:68). Yet Dallas is not just a city of native Blacks and Whites; as of 1996, between eight and nine percent of the city's population was foreign born (Brettell, Cordell, and Hollifield 1996). Foreign-born persons are from a wide range of places, including Somalia, Ethiopia, Nigeria, Syria, Iran, India, Cambodia, Laos, Vietnam, Korea, Taiwan, Russia, Samoa, Tonga, El Salvador, and Guatemala, among others. Taking note of this diversity in 1995, the *Dallas Morning News* ran a series called "Immigration: The Changing Face of Dallas," which examined the benefits and challenges of the new Dallas. According to the 2000 census, 65.5 percent of the over 5 million residents of the Dallas–Fort Worth Metroplex were White, about 14 percent were Black, and about 22 percent Hispanic. Mexicans are by far the most numerous group within the "Hispanic" category; they alone constitute about 17 percent of the total population.

Historically, Dallas has been a bastion of White power. The city was incorporated in 1856 and had no Black or Latino elected official until 1969. Even then, this was merely a form of tokenism because the real power-holders in Dallas were the business elite, who were all White (Achor 1991:59). Only in the past decade or so has Dallas become a place where Whites have begun to share power with African-Americans, Latinos, and other non-White groups—although the White leadership has not given up power without a struggle. Although by the 1990s, the police force, city council, mayor's office, and other city agencies had been diversified and had significant minority representation, racial tensions have not disappeared. Most notable is the extreme racial tension not only between Whites and minorities but also between Latinos and African-Americans. In 1995 an African-American mayor, Ron Kirk, was elected for the first time in Dallas history. Kirk's moderate views appealed to constituents of all colors and backgrounds. Yet city politics, especially in the Dallas Independent School District (DISD), have been an embarrassment to many leaders because of the vicious racial politicking among the district's leadership.

The DISD student body is predominantly African-American and Latino and, as of 1993, less than fifteen percent White. In 1993, despite monitoring by a federal court, the DISD was still not officially desegregated (Payne 1994:412). The district has created magnet schools to attract White students and help alleviate segregation. It has also hired minority administrators and teachers. But as is so common in Dallas, the DISD has been a battleground not just between Whites and minorities but between African-Americans and Latinos. When in 1997 African-American protesters scuffled with Latinos at school board meetings, Mayor Kirk was quick to denounce the violence and call for charges to be pressed against anyone who engaged in violent acts at meetings (Lopez and Gillman 1997). Lee Alcorn, then the president of the local NAACP, was incensed by what he viewed as the mayor's lack of support: "The mayor needs to keep his nose out of school board business. Protests made it possible for his Black face to be on the council" (Lopez and Gillman 1997). Things reached a particularly low point when the newly elected superintendent of schools, Yvonne González, was accused of using $16,000 of DISD money to buy furniture for her personal use. This gave African-Americans ammunition against Latinos and heightened ethnic tensions in Dallas. Many Latinos defended her, claiming that she was a victim of racial politics. Eventually found guilty of the charges, González was forced to return the money, lost her teaching certification, and was sent to prison for fifteen months. Latino leaders viewed the incident as a step backward.

How do these kinds of tensions affect Yucatecans? Take the case of Parkland, a charity-based, public, county hospital that principally serves those in Dallas County who lack medical insurance. Most Yucatecans count on Parkland for some or all of their medical needs. Not only is Parkland close to where the migrants live, but it is also not necessary to provide social security numbers or other documentation of legal residence. In fact, almost all of the Yucatecan women who have given birth in Dallas have delivered there.

The politics of race are virulent at Parkland, where, in 1995, African-American county commissioner John Wiley Price, along with others, was daily picketing the entrance to protest what they considered to be inequities in hiring and promotions of African-Americans. For his part, Chairman Pat Cotton countered by stating that if the hospital needed improvement in any area it was in the hiring of more Hispanic and bilingual employees (Beil 1995), highlighting the competition for scarce resources between Blacks and Latinos. Whatever the debate, the fact is that the Yucatecans had to cross the picket line in order to secure medical care.

That Yucatecans live in a racially charged environment has undoubtedly shaped their attitudes towards African-Americans. The Yucatecans have frequent contacts with poor and working-class African-Americans although they do not live in a Black residential neighborhood. For the most part, Yucatecans' views of the African-Americans with whom they interact are negative. They identify with other Latinos in Dallas as a result of a common language and common preoccupation with immigration issues, and thus are sympathetic to the Latino community's struggle for scarce resources, which pits them against African-Americans. Yucatecans also view African-Americans as prone to go on welfare, and they cannot understand why African-Americans would accept government support rather than getting jobs. From their perspective, the United States offers enormous economic opportunity and it is illogical not to take advantage of it.

Yucatecans exhibit prejudice towards other groups as well, notably the several Vietnamese families living in their apartment complex. On several occasions, I overheard Yucatecans making fun of the Vietnamese language and complaining about the strange and foreign culinary smells emanating from their apartments. The Vietnamese are culturally even more different from the American mainstream than they are and of a similar or lower socioeconomic level. Interestingly, Yucatecans are fairly tolerant of the vocal and politically active gay community nearby. I suspect that this is because members of the gay community are mostly White, and the Yucatecans afford respect to anyone who is, in their terminology, "*americano.*"

What about relations with other Mexicans? Mexicans began migrating to Dallas during the railroad boom at the beginning of the twentieth century, and another surge occurred during and after the Mexican Revolution. By the 1920s, Mexican migrants were a sizable ethnic minority in Dallas (Corchado and Trejo 1999:3). The 1986 Immigration Reform and Control Act, which granted amnesty to over 3.1

million immigrants throughout the United States (most of them Mexican), has further entrenched the Mexican migrant presence in Dallas (Ibid:5). In 2000 about 890,000 Mexicans lived in the Dallas–Fort Worth Metroplex, and, as one scholar observes, the number "continues to grow, grow, grow with no end in sight" (Ibid:1).

Dallas has attracted migrants from all across Mexico, the most numerous group coming from the state of Guanajuato in central Mexico (Ibid:6). A list from the Mexican Consulate in Dallas shows that there are 33 mutual aid associations from eight states: Aguascalientes (1), Durango (2), Guanajuato (8), Guerrero (2), Hidalgo (4), San Luis Potosí (14), Yucatán (1), and Zacatecas (2).

Yucatecans from Kaal are familiar with Yucatecans in Dallas from other parts of Yucatán. In one apartment complex close to where the Kaaleños live, there are several families from a town close to Kaal in Northern Yucatán. The migration from this town began before the migration from Kaal and the migrant population exceeds that from Kaal, although it is less residentially concentrated. One family from this town owns a restaurant/bakery called Chichén Itzá, which now has several branches in the Dallas Metroplex. Those from Kaal, however, constitute the largest residentially concentrated group of Yucatecans in Dallas.

Given the large Mexican migration, it is not surprising that Dallas has a distinctively Mexican flavor. The Yucatecans are comfortable with other Mexican migrants and interact with them on the job (for men) and in Spanish-speaking business establishments and social service agencies that they patronize. Some Yucatecan men and women have developed friendships with people from other parts of Mexico. Nevertheless, the Kaaleños live and work together and spend most of their time with other Yucatecos.

THE YUCATECANS IN DALLAS

It is summer in Dallas, oppressively hot for even native Dallasites, but not for Yucatecans. To the contrary, it is the cold winter in North Texas that

Yucatecans consider unbearable. Summertime is nice and hot, just like the Yucatán, and it is when the parents of the migrants prefer to visit their children in Dallas. Doña Lola is in town, and she has brought spices and medicines from Yucatán, as well as letters from migrants' family-members in Kaal. She wears a beautiful *huipil* at all times, and she spends her time in her daughter's apartment, cooking, and chatting with people who have come to pick up the letters she has brought from Mexico. She loves sightseeing, and her children take her around on their days off. Next week she will go to a Texas Rangers game with her children and grandchildren. She enjoys her visits to Dallas, and is grateful that she has been able to procure a tourist visa and that her children can afford to send for her every summer. Her daughter and two of her three sons are undocumented, so it is cheaper and easier for her to visit Dallas than for them to go to Kaal. Her husband remains in Yucatán—someone has to tend to the animals and the *milpa*. Maybe he will come next year...

This excerpt from my fieldnotes begins to give a sense of the lives of Yucatecans in Dallas. At any given time there are approximately 200 people from Kaal in Dallas, and I interviewed about half of them. Some basic facts about the people I interviewed are worth noting. The Yucatecans in Dallas are young. Most are between the ages of 20 and 30. Of the 37 women and 63 men I spoke with, 59 percent were married, 11 percent were in a consensual union, 25 percent were single, and 5 percent were divorced, separated, or widowed. Of the married individuals, three quarters had their spouses with them in Dallas and a quarter had a spouse in Mexico. Sixty-five percent of those with children had all of their children with them in Dallas. Almost a quarter had left behind all their children in Mexico and eleven percent had some children with them in Dallas and others in Mexico. Both men and women had a similar level of education, slightly more than half having finished at least some middle school. About a third had only completed some elementary school. Several women had no schooling at all. Of the remaining one hundred Yucatecan migrants whom I did not interview, the majority are men. These men live in apartments with many other men—sometimes as many as twelve in a two-bedroom apartment. They live an uncomfortable life in Dallas and remit most of their earnings to their families in Kaal. A large majority of these men are undocumented.

Legal Status

Lupe just had a car accident and she is frustrated and angry. Her car is in bad shape and her friend Melba, who was sitting in the passenger seat, has a sore neck. Lupe was driving in the parking lot of a popular pizza restaurant when a Spanish-speaking Mexican man rear-ended her with his car. He apologized, promised to pay for it, and gave her his phone number. She was relieved that he did not want to call the police, because she is undocumented and has no car insurance. When she later called the number that the man gave her, she found that he had given her a false name and number. What could she do? Once again, her undocumented status had left her helpless.

Because it affects so many aspects of their lives, legal status is a crucial issue for Yucatecans. It is not just a matter of limiting their employment options. Undocumented status causes all kinds of other problems for the migrants. Getting driver's licenses, automobile insurance, round trip airplane tickets, apartment leases, or bank accounts are all difficult, if not impossible, for undocumented immigrants. Almost three quarters of the Yucatecans I interviewed were undocumented. Taking account the one hundred or so men whom I did not interview, I estimate that about 90 percent of the total population is undocumented.

Yucatecans do want legal residency. But because most Yucatecans arrived in the United States between 1992 and 1998, few could take advantage of the 1986 IRCA amnesty and obtain legal status for themselves. Undocumented migrants without immediate relatives in the United States who are legal permanent residents are extremely unlikely to be able to legalize their status unless there is a change in U.S. immigration law. So, most of the undocumented Yucatecans in Dallas have little hope of adjusting their residency status.

Work/Employment

A new restaurant is opening in Dallas and it is on a bus route. A group of Yucatecan men go to fill out applications. Although none of the men have legal

This is the citizenship ceremony of one of the few Yucatecans to become a U.S. citizen.

residency, all have some sort of false documentation and restaurant experience. The men get hired as dishwashers, busboys, and cooks. They will start this weekend. Other Yucatecan men hear about their success and a few more go to apply. The longer they stay at this job, the more Yucatecan men will apply there; and whenever the chef is looking for a new employee, the men will recruit fellow Yucatecans for the position.

Mona is desperate for a job. Her husband is drinking again, and was fired from his good restaurant job as a result. She is tired of having to depend on an unreliable husband. She wants to clean houses— but she does not want the responsibility of taking care of other people's children. She circles ads in the newspaper and asks me to make the calls. I call, but we are both discouraged by the high demands of the employers. (Does she have a car? Does she speak English? Can she baby-sit my infant while she cleans my house? Can she live-in?) Weeks later she finally gets a job cleaning a house twice a week after an acquaintance on the bus gives her a phone number of a woman in search of domestic help. Mona works hard cleaning her house for several months and the woman recommends her to friends. Before long she has cleaning jobs five days a week. Her husband's alcoholism ultimately leads him down a self-destructive path and he is eventually put in jail for violating probation. Mona is now completely economically self-sufficient.

As these two vignettes indicate, the Yucatecans in Dallas have found their niche in the low end of the city's service industries. Men work in restaurants and hotels, and most employed women—about two-thirds of the women I interviewed—work as domestics. Luxury hotels and restaurants are plentiful in Dallas. Hotels cater to visiting business people who come to Dallas to go to one of the wholesale markets, or to attend conferences and conventions at one of the many convention halls and hotels. Restaurants, of the trendiest variety, are abundant. These restaurants and hotels are located close to the Yucatecans' homes and it is here that nearly all the men are employed. Most men work behind the scenes, starting out as dishwashers, moving up to become busboys or preparation cooks and then, if they are lucky, ending up as line cooks or sous chefs. Dallas restaurants are usually only successful for a short time; when a new one opens up, the trend-conscious clientele moves on to a new "find." As a result, Yucatecans frequently change jobs. And there is another factor. Men will often quit a job in order to visit Mexico to participate in fiestas or other important celebrations in Kaal. When they return to Dallas they find a job in a new place without mentioning why they left their last job. Because low-level positions are hard to fill, restaurateurs are desperate to hire new people. Chefs rely on social networks among migrants to fill positions. If a good worker recommends a friend or relative, he is likely to be hired. For this reason most restaurants where Yucatecans work have other Yucatecans employed there as well. Of all the Yucatecan men I spoke to, 85 percent had at least one Yucatecan coworker at their place of employment.

Few of the men receive benefits such as health or dental insurance or paid vacations. Typically, small owner-run restaurants do not offer these benefits, although they pay better than chain restaurants or hotels, which do. It is hard for an undocumented person to find employment at hotel or chain restaurants, which are stricter in screening potential employees. Yucatecans who work in hotel restaurants are legal immigrants who accept lower wages in exchange for the attractive benefits package and job security offered. The average income reported by the men surveyed in the late 1990s was $7.09 per hour; there was almost no difference between men with legal permission to work ($7.05) and for undocumented workers ($7.12).

As for women, few work in restaurants and those who do generally work in fast food establishments, where they average $5.12 per hour. Most women work *en casa* (as domestics), cleaning homes or taking care of small children.

Women are more likely than men to work off the books. Their pay is not taxed and it is given to them in cash. The average hourly wage of Yucatecan domestics in the late 1990s was $7.25. Job security and working conditions are largely contingent on the personality of their *patrona* (boss). Most women are pleased with their jobs although a few complained about not receiving raises or not being paid for a working day when a *patrona* calls to cancel. Women are constantly on the lookout for new houses to clean, reading newspaper ads, talking to friends and acquaintances, and listening to a morning radio program that announces employment opportunities.

Some women work for office cleaning companies, but these jobs are not considered desirable because the hours (5:00–10:30 p.m.) conflict with childrearing responsibilities and the pay (average $4.37 per hour) is poor. Women prefer to work during school hours, leaving them time to care for children after school and on weekends. Those who work in the evening or on weekends leave their children with family members or pay one of several Yucatecan women to watch children in their homes. A few women work in clothing factories or bus tables at the convention center during large events. The average income reported for all women is $6.52 per hour, which is 57 cents less per hour than what men earn. In general, women are also much less likely than men to find jobs through Yucatecan friends and relatives.

Several teenagers have after-school jobs. The boys work in restaurants where their fathers are employed. Two sisters work at a local clothing store that caters to a Latino clientele. There is a high value placed on working and young people generally want to help their families and earn cash to buy things they want such as fancy sneakers, compact discs, and fast food.

Because Yucatecans live close to where they work, most either walk to work or take the bus. The wealthy neighborhood to the immediate east of their homes and the restaurants in their own neighborhood offer a wide selection of employment. At the time of research, work was easy to find, but it may well be that during the recession of 2001, jobs were harder to come by.

Local Spaces

It is a Sunday afternoon at Villatree apartment complex and little Jennifer's 2nd birthday. Her Yucatecan migrant parents are throwing her a party. As the mostly Yucatecan guests enter the apartment they hand Jennifer's mother a gift, which she displays on a table along with the others. Jennifer's parents instruct the guests to take a seat on one of the mismatched chairs, borrowed from neighbors, that encircle the room. The guests are offered a beer or soda and handed a plate of food. Outside, a crowd of Yucatecan men gathers in the parking lot drinking beer. The music in the apartment is loud, limiting conversation. All the while, groups of children run in and out of the apartment, screaming in delight. There is a *piñata* hanging over a tree near the parking lot, and the children are looking forward to smashing it and eating its contents. As the day goes on, some guests leave and others arrive. A few couples get up and dance a *cumbia*. The hosts are delighted that people are dancing—it is the hallmark of a successful Yucatecan party. Jennifer's father runs back and forth, delivering beer and plates of food to the large group of men who are still out in the parking lot. Like clockwork, at 10:00 p.m., the police arrive to break up the party. If the music is turned down and the crowd disperses in the parking lot, the celebration will continue, but most of the guests start to leave. Hopefully, the apartment manager won't find out about the party. She has prohibited such gatherings, but it is a Sunday and she is not around. Besides, this is a first offense for Jennifer's parents.

The "Villatree" apartment complex is the place where most Yucatecans from Kaal have lived since the mid-1980s. Virtually all newcomers live there when they first come to Dallas, and only later (and sometimes not at all) do they relocate to other nearby apartment complexes. Almost all Yucatecans from Kaal live within walking distance of one another.

As a result, they shop in the same stores, eat in the same restaurants, use the same bus routes, and go to the same schools and churches, and many work in the same places. Brookhaven, the Dallas neighborhood where the apartment complex is located, is extremely diverse. A vocal gay and lesbian community is located in Brookhaven and gay bars and nightclubs line the main strip, where parades and celebrations of gay pride are common. Members of the gay community tend to be well off, but Brookhaven also has pockets of working-class and poor Latinos and Vietnamese, as well as businesses such as a "Dollar Store" (where nothing is priced over a dollar), supermarkets aimed at Latino consumers, money transfer places, *taquerías*, and discount stores. The median per capita income of the census tract where most Kaaleños live was a low $12,481 according to the 1990 census, with median family income at $23,678. Brookhaven is predominantly made up of apartment complexes, condominiums, and renovated old houses that contain two or more separate apartments. Well-off residents of Brookhaven live in condominiums and house-based apartments; Latinos and Vietnamese live in apartment complexes.

Villatree mostly caters to Latino and a few Vietnamese renters. The Mexican-American manager is highly suspicious of inquiries from English speakers as I discovered when I called to ask about the availability of an apartment for a Yucatecan looking for a place to live. The apartment complex is poorly maintained. Cockroaches abound, and maintenance problems go unresolved for months. Often, air conditioning and heating are out of service, clearly related to the fact that utilities are included in the rent. Residents are frightened to complain too vociferously to management because of the difficulties involved in finding another apartment without legal documentation and a good credit history. In 1998, the rent was $550 a month for an apartment with two bedrooms and two bathrooms, including utilities—a low rent by Dallas standards. Villatree is close to two bus routes, making it relatively easy to get around Dallas without a car. Less than a quarter of the Yucatecans have cars and those who do are constantly asked to taxi people around. Most people use the bus even if they have access to a car.

Shopping is within walking distance to Villatree. Two supermarkets cater to a Latino customer base and are easily accessible as are two pharmacies and several inexpensive restaurants that Yucatecans frequent. The elementary and middle schools are both about a half a mile away so that students can walk to class. The high school requires a bus trip. Some of the men play soccer at one of the two nearby parks every Sunday, calling their team "Los Mayas." Yucatecan men also go to a cantina close to the apartment complex.

On early weekday mornings, Villatree is quiet; children are at school and men are sleeping late after a long night at work. By afternoon the apartment complex is a lively, family-oriented place. Children play in the parking lots outside their apartments, and women sit on the doorsteps minding them. There is music and a flurry of activity. Sometimes teenagers pass by in loud "lowrider" or other similarly flashy automobiles. People are out walking to go to the store or the bus stops or to visit neighbors. In the early evening there is a similar buzz of activity, especially in the summer months when it does not get dark until after 8:30 p.m.

On weekends and some weekday nights men assemble in Villatree's parking lot to drink beer. Often they begin drinking in one apartment. Inevitably, they move outside to the *calle* (street), where they find it easier to speak out of the earshot of women and children. Since many of the restaurants where men work are closed on Sunday and Monday, these drinking binges most often occur on Saturday and Sunday nights, but they happen during the week as well. The women tiptoe around these gatherings so as not to attract the attention of any of the drunken participants. Thus by day and by night there is a different atmosphere in the apartment complex. At night women and children gather inside apartments whereas men prefer to be outside. Women are mobile at night but use a buddy system so that they are not forced to walk alone. The days feel safer and both men and women walk around freely.

Even those Yucatecans who do not live in Villatree tend to visit and spend time there. A number have gone to live elsewhere out of frustration with the poor management or because of conflicts with others from Kaal. Moving to another apartment complex allows them to maintain some distance from other Yucatecans without altogether cutting ties. The other neighboring apartment complexes where Yucatecans live are generally occupied exclusively by Latino renters. Only a few Yucatecans have purchased houses; all of the homeowners are legal residents and still visit the central complex on a regular basis. One family has bought a home in a small residential neighborhood directly behind the apartment complex. Two other families live in the suburbs; they too maintain close contact with the Yucatecans in the central complex.

CONCLUSION

Dallas is the principal receiving area in the United States for Kaaleños. Employment in the low-end service sector in Dallas is readily available, and the compensation is higher than in Kaal. In Dallas the Yucatecos live and work close to one another and, both individually and collectively, maintain close ties to Kaal. As will become clear, Dallas can be viewed as an extension of Kaal. Though spatially distant, Dallas and Kaal are connected symbolically and materially by flows of people, goods, and information.

4

Crossing the Line: Migrants and the U.S.-Mexico Border

Ever since the U.S. government has regulated the political boundary between the United States and Mexico, crossing the border has had symbolic importance to migrants. The experience itself has been canonized in Mexican music and popular culture. A brief listen to most Latino radio stations reveals Mexican songs (most are of a rural musical genre called *corridos* and *rancheras*), describing the adventures of those who dare to cross the line and confront *la migra* (INS). The *telenovela* (soap opera) *Camila,* broadcast via Univision in both Mexico and the United States, concluded with the main male character, a well educated Mexican lawyer, having to cross over *mojado* (undocumented) with working class migrants. In another recent *telenovela, Amigas y Rivales*, a character (Nayeli) flees to Los Angeles in the back of a tractor trailer when she runs up against murderous criminals who have her on a hit list. When the border patrol searches the truck and discovers the hidden human cargo, Nayeli flees once again. She makes it to Los Angeles where she becomes completely dependent on others for the basic necessities of life. These plot lines highlight the drama that is reality for many Mexicans who come to the United States.

The border between Mexico and the United States is symbolically important for citizens of both nations.

U.S. Migration Law, Border Crossing, and Transnational Migration

Legal status is crucial to a discussion of transnational migration because it affects the relative difficulty or ease of leaving the United States in order to maintain ties to home areas. Those without documents and a reasonable possibility of legalizing their status may not be concerned about breaking rules established by U.S. law and enforced by the Immigration and Naturalization Service (INS).

Under U.S. law, upon arrival in this country all migrants are classified as occupying a particular migration status, which determines their rights and obligations under U.S. law. I use the term *undocumented* for any migrant who is in the United States without proper immigration documentation. According to U.S. law, those who do not have permission to enter the country and do so surreptitiously are classified as Entered without Inspection (EWI) and are Present without Admission (PWA). They are technically not even allowed to be in the United States. Those who cross the border illegally or, in the case of many non-Mexicans, enter by boat, plane, or train, fall into this category. Others have tourist or student visas that permit them to be in the U.S. for a specified period of time, but prohibit them from employment. These visas are difficult to obtain. To get one, a person must prove that he or she has assets in Mexico (or other country of origin) and therefore does not pose a risk for overstaying his or her visa. When immigrants do overstay these visas, they are also undocumented, even though they did not have to cross the border illegally to gain entry. Legal permanent residents (holders of the popularly known "green card," now called a MICA) and naturalized U.S. citizens are permitted to both live and work in the United States. They may travel and return to the United States without many problems—although legal permanent residents cannot stay out of the United States for longer than a six-month period without the risk of losing legal residency status. Although the Immigration Reform and Control Act (IRCA) of 1986 granted legal amnesty to millions of (mostly Mexican) undocumented migrants in the United States who could prove that they were living and working in the United States for a specified period before 1986, this law had little impact on Yucatecans who mostly came after 1986. Moreover, subsequent legislation passed in 1996, the Illegal Immigration Reform and Immigrant Responsibility Act (IIRIRA), has made it even more difficult for undocumented immigrants to legalize their residency status in the U.S. People who migrated after 1986 and do not have close relatives in the United States currently have no possibilities of legalizing their status. Prior to the September 11, 2001, tragedy, Presidents Vicente Fox and George Bush were discussing the possibility of another amnesty that would legalize millions of undocumented Mexicans in the United States. These plans have been tabled as a result of the terrorist attacks. Only time will tell if there will again be an amnesty.

Transnational migrants occupy various legal statuses. Legal permanent residents or U.S. citizens can most easily travel back and forth between the United States and their native countries. Undocumented migrants have the most difficulty visiting home; their return is expensive and dangerous.

Indeed, it is truly remarkable how transnationalism can flourish even among populations, like the Yucatecan migrants in Dallas, which are predominately undocumented.

THE BORDER CROSSING PROCESS

Ever since the migration from Kaal to Texas began in 1969 it has followed a common pattern—one which is the same for first time migrants as for those who frequently make the journey. The first part of the process requires social networking. In order to go to the United States it is necessary to find someone to pay for the trip and, especially in the case of women and children, someone to accompany them along the way. The most popular time for people to leave for the United States is right after one of the two annual religious fiestas in Kaal. There are always migrants visiting home for the fiesta and people know that they will be returning to Texas. Relatives in Texas often make arrangements for their kin to cross with these returning migrants. Men without relatives in the United States find others to help. The point is that such help is needed to make the trip. The *coyote's* (border smuggler's) fee, around $1,800 in 2002, does not include expenses incurred to get to the border from Yucatán. This is a huge sum to people in Kaal, and those migrating for the first time (or after a long stay back in Mexico) must find someone to defray the cost. Almost always the sponsors are migrants in the United States who send money with the expectation that the newcomer will soon find employment and pay them back. Often, but not always, the sponsors are relatives. These sponsorships create bonds of patronage between a border crosser and an established migrant. Thus, first and foremost, migrants are indebted to their sponsors (i.e. their patrons) (cf. Adler 2002).

Once the monetary arrangements have been worked out, a group of men, sometimes accompanied by a few women and children, travel to Mérida. From there an airplane or bus is taken to Mexico City. In Mexico City, another bus or plane is taken to the large border city where everyone heading to Dallas prefers to cross. Once there the group locates a hotel and the *coyote/a* is contacted and paid. Sometimes the *coyote* collects the payment directly from the migrant's sponsor when the group reaches Texas. Yucatecans tend to employ the same several *coyotes* over and over again because relationships of trust have been established. The *coyote* decides when the migrants will cross. Sometimes (s)he is ready to cross the very next day and other times (s)he will insist on waiting as long as two weeks. All depends on the *coyote's* observations; if the border patrol is particularly vigilant (s)he may prefer to wait it out.

When the first attempt is made, the *coyote* and his or her assistants instruct the migrants. If there is a large group, they separate into smaller groups before crossing. If successful they meet at a location on the U.S. side designated by the *coyote*. The *coyote* organizes the dangerous exit out of the U.S. border town, which is often the most risky part. In most cases the migrants are given airplane, train, or bus tickets and instructed on how to behave so as not to be viewed as "suspicious" by authorities. A trip to the store is often necessary to purchase U.S.-style clothing that will camouflage their undocumented status. In other cases, migrants are piled into the trunks of cars or the cabins of tractor-trailers. Several migrants said they had been in the trunk of a car, with as many as three others, for several hours at a time. One man described how he and 17 other migrants (from other places besides Yucatán) traveled from the border to north Texas in the cargo area of a tractor-trailer. The walls were made of metal and there was only a vent for air. They were fine until the truck had to stop for a long stretch of time. Because the truck was not moving, air did not pass through the vents:

> The air ran out. It was then that I saw that the girl started to pass out. The truck had four fiber glass portals so that the light could enter; they weren't for air, they were for light... And then I saw that her father also started to pass out.... a man who was with them—I don't know where he was from—took off his belt buckle—you know the Mexicans wear a big belt buckle—and said 'let's break this thing so that air can get in here.' 'No! You are going to make a lot of noise.' 'This girl is going to die. Let's all get off then and run like hell and whoever makes it

makes it.... no, no, we are going to break this' and he started to break holes in the fiberglass like five inches.... and the other man put his nose there so that he could breathe and his daughter too. The water that we had, we splashed on the daughter so that she would come to and she reacted to that but her father did not. And then I noticed another girl also, and then another and one went running to get to the little hole and pushed the man aside and she was holding on because she began to faint too. And because there was no wind and because the hole was bigger inside the truck than outside.... I made a tube out of cardboard and put it in the hole so that the air could enter. And the man fell down.... and all the water we had we splashed on him. And almost all of the women were starting to pass out and one started to pray for her husband. The man started to die. It was dramatic. It was very dangerous.

If, in this first attempt at crossing, anyone in the group is unfortunate enough to get caught by the INS they will be taken in for processing and sent back to Mexico. The unlucky ones have to find the *coyote* and go through the crossing ordeal once more. One couple was not successful until the fourth attempt. The wife tells of the experience:

We passed over the first time...and we were in [border city] and we ran because we saw a border patrol truck. We ran and they saw that we were running. And we arrived in a little park.... This time when we were running there were two girls running with us. And we ran so that we could lose them [the INS] but they saw us and caught us. They asked us where we were going and we told them that we were from here. And they said 'Is that true? Show us your papers.' And we did not have anything. 'I am sorry but you will have to come with us in the truck.' And after that they sent us back to Mexico. One of the girls that was running with us stayed there [in the U.S.] because when she got to the park she began to walk as if nothing was happening and she got to a public telephone and pretended that she was talking on the phone. They didn't catch her.... We waited two more hours and the *coyote* said that we were going to try it again. This time we again crossed over in the water.... we passed through a different spot this time. When we crossed over the wire we had to cross over train tracks...there we all crossed running. From there he told us that we would meet in a bus station. But at the same time a helicopter passed overhead and they saw us. And I think that they called and reported us to a car on the ground. We made it seem like we were there buying tickets. We waited on line but they did not believe us and once again they told us that we had to go with them.... We were back in Mexico and it was night and we waited until the following day. The next day we passed over the same way.... from there we went to a McDonald's. And the *coyote* began to explain how we can do it and we ate and we went on a bus and arrived at the airport.... The *coyote* bought the tickets for the airplane and gave them to us and explained what we should do. 'Don't be nervous so that they don't notice you.' And we separated, my husband and I, although we were going to travel on the same flight.... When they announced that they were boarding I went to stand in line to give my ticket and a woman came up to me. I saw that she came up and took my ticket; she said, '*Juana Sosa*, is this your ticket? Are you traveling alone?' And I said, 'No, I am traveling with my husband but he is not here right now.' And then she took out her wallet and told me she was INS.

Some give up after a failed first crossing attempt. Others are determined to join their relatives and friends in Texas, and will try again and again until they finally cross successfully. It is not unusual for a few unlucky people from a group, the rest of whom have successfully crossed, to spend three or four additional weeks at the border in repeated attempts to cross.

Among another, smaller community of Kaaleños in the San Bernardino valley of California, the border crossing experience is also of great significance. I spoke with one woman there, Elsa, who had a particularly harrowing experience involving, among other things, separation from her young son. It is difficult for undocumented adults to cross over with their own children owing to the physical challenges of the journey and the tendency for young children to cry and talk loudly at inopportune times. *Coyotes* often separate children from their parents in order to cross them over via other, safer means. The INS is generally less suspicious of young children and so *coyotes* (who often have U.S. residency themselves) usually put them in a group with their own children. In this case, Elsa, a 20-year-old woman from Kaal, was making her first trip to the United States with her young son. Her husband, who paid for her trip, waited for her in California. Elsa left Kaal and flew to a border city with her son and another man from Kaal. They left on a Monday and arrived in the border city at about 6:00 p.m. When they arrived they could not find the *coyota* who was supposed to meet them at the airport. Elsa had very little money and the young man accompanying her had no money at all. They found a taxi and paid for a hotel room. In a panic, Elsa called her husband in California, who contacted a Yucatecan man living in the border city; the man collected the three of them at the hotel and put them up in his home for a few days. Elsa's husband called the *coyota*, who was selected because she specializes in getting children across the border. The *coyota* took the child from his mother on Friday—he was screaming in protest—and crossed over successfully on the first attempt. He was taken to his father in California. With the phone number of another *coyote* in hand (an associate of the woman who crossed her son), early Saturday morning Elsa and another man from Kaal took a bus to a different border city to meet him. They spent several days in what Elsa called a *hacienda* (a house with a lot of land in a rural area) before they attempted—unsuccessfully—to cross over the border through the river:

> We passed over, and at first the water came up to our knees. We took off our shoes and socks and put

them in a plastic bag and I was holding on to the young man because the water was pulling me so I had to hold on. When we were in the water the *migra* came and told us to get out of the water. '*Carajo*, get out of the water' they said and 'hold on to the young woman; don't let her get away.' They told me to get into the truck and they checked the men for papers and they had to get in too.... They took us for processing and took our photos and fingerprints and they left us there for four hours and I was really wet.... it was really cold. They caught us at 4:00 p.m. and we didn't leave until 9:00. We called them at the hacienda and they came to pick us up.

Three days later they tried again. This time the strategy was to climb the border fence. According to Elsa, it was very high and she was frightened:

We had to jump up but I couldn't because it was really high. And the *coyote* told me 'Hurry up, nobody is around' and I started to climb up and they helped me and I reached the top. Then they wanted me to jump but I didn't want to because I was afraid I would get hurt. They yelled, 'jump! jump!' and I jumped and I did not get hurt. They told me to run and I ran but two border patrol trucks came right away. I was running and the men with me shouted 'go back! go back!' and I went running back [to the Mexican side of the border]. I was so afraid; it's like I forgot everything. I climbed up and jumped down again. The *migra* stayed there watching us. If I had been just a little bit slower they would have caught me.

They returned to spend three days at the hacienda before trying again. Elsa had already called her husband (collect) twice and knew that her son had arrived safely, but he was constantly crying for his mother. This made Elsa more anxious and the wait was miserable. The third attempt was through the river. (In the meantime, the young man from

Kaal had crossed the border with a false ID card.) This time Elsa crossed over with another young woman.

> The third time we had passed the river and the canal and we were running and that is when they caught us. We had run a lot and we couldn't run any more; I was so tired. They told us to stop and it was getting dark so they shone their lights on us and we got into the truck again. We had to go in for processing and we did not get out until midnight. We called the lady and they came to get us again.

After waiting another several days, the *coyote* took them to another border city and once again tried to get them to climb the border fence.

> This time I couldn't do it because this fence was even higher and it was right in the middle of the city. All the people were watching us and I said to the *coyote*—and he was a little drunk—that there is no way I can do it. I cannot climb this fence. And there was another young man with us and he said that he couldn't do it either. The lady [*coyota*] who was going to take us up north was waiting on the other side, but I said you know what, I am not going to be able to climb this fence; it is too high, I can't do it. We went back to the house again.

About three weeks had already passed since she arrived at the border. In the fifth and final attempt Elsa, another young woman, and a *coyote* walked through the night, leaving at 10:30 p.m. It was cold and they walked for hours. On the way the *coyote* saw the border patrol and they lay down to hide:

> We walked and walked and at 3:45 we were almost at the highway. And I said 'there is the Border Patrol' and the van stopped and they shone the lights in our direction. We dropped to the ground immediately and I said, 'they are going to come for us'; I was sure that they were coming for us. But then they left! They left! The *coyote* said 'quick' and we got up real-

ly quick and started to run...We got to the highway
and found the *coyota* waiting in her van on the other
side. Quickly, the girl crossed the highway first and
got in the van and the lady said, 'Tell the other one to
come fast' and I ran across the highway to where she
was parked. I got in and we made it.

After being taken to the house of a man on the U.S. side of
the border, another *coyote* came that evening to take her to
the San Bernardino valley. Before they could leave, they had
to see whether the border patrol had established any check-
points in the area. When the coast was clear, Elsa was taken
to see her husband. She arrived at 2:00 in the morning. After
almost three weeks at the border, she finally made it.

Border crossing may be glamorized as an adventure in
Mexican popular culture, but, to border crossers themselves, it creates fear and ambivalence. Border crossers with
money are vulnerable to theft. Those without money are at
risk because they must rely on and trust *coyotes* to take care
of them while on their journey. As the examples offered here
make clear, the experience can be truly terrifying, and separation from family, helplessness, discomfort, and dependence on strangers are regular parts of the process.

EFFECTS OF BORDER CROSSING

The border crossing experience and the public storytelling
that follows have several effects. First, the border crossing
experience serves as a type of community "glue" that binds
migrants together and helps establish community boundaries. The border crossing experience is difficult and risky
but it enables migrants to join kinsmen and friends in the
United States. The crossing of the border symbolically represents the willingness of individuals to sacrifice for others in
the community. The hardship endured is emphasized in the
telling because it shows how much the migrants will do for
their fellow townsmen. News of border crossings spreads
rapidly among migrants in Dallas (and California) as well as
among families left behind in Yucatán. When migrants
reach the border city, they call relatives (who are often their

sponsors) in the United States and let them know of their progress. Once a phone call has been made, this information travels quickly on both sides of the border. If it is taking an unusually long time for the migrants to cross, they call the United States frequently in order to calm the nerves of those anxiously awaiting their safe arrival.

Those in the "audience" watching the border crossing process from the relative safety of their homes discuss at length, with all who will listen, the experiences of the border crossers. The crossing experience becomes the major topic of conversation among Yucatecan migrants in Texas. If women and children are crossing, the topic is even more highly charged and filled with drama.

Sponsors make it known to all in the community that they have paid for the journey of the soon-to-arrive migrant. Indeed, sponsorship is a source of great prestige, and it is considered an honor to pay for another's passage, especially if the person crossing has a position of wealth or prestige in Kaal.

When the migrants finally arrive there is much discussion of the details of their border crossing experience. These stories are told and repeated over and over again in conversation, on the telephone, and in letters. People on both sides of the border find these stories to be compelling, and never tire of hearing the details.

Border crossing clearly divides those who migrate and those who do not. Many migrants said that when they visit Kaal they often feel like outsiders. Although they still consider themselves to be part of the Kaal community, they say that their migrant status has changed them. Although their migrant status is definitely a mark of prestige in Kaal, it can also make them feel uncomfortable and "different" in the context of the Kaal community. At the same time, the border crossing experience is a principal criterion for membership in the migrant community. In telling their stories to non-migrants and perhaps encouraging them to take a trip to the United States, border crossers are inviting others to take part in the transnational experience. When non-migrants feel that they too can be migrants, a bond is reestablished.

Border crossing also establishes powerful ties of obligation between migrants and their sponsors. Whoever pays for the passage earns prestige in the community and the loyalty of the recipient. Newcomers to the United States rely on established migrants for money, papers, material goods, or a place to live, all of which creates dependence at the very onset of arrival. These debts must be paid immediately in order to save face within the community.

BORDER CROSSING: "WEAPON OF THE WEAK"

Political borders are regulated, usually by force, by agents of nation-states. The U.S.-Mexico border is particularly striking because of the socioeconomic differences between the two countries. Yet, people from Mexico cross every day to shop, work, visit family and friends, and live in the United States, just as U.S. citizens cross the border into Mexico for shopping, vacation, and adventure. Many of the thousands who cross every day are doing so legally with border crossing cards and visas.

But every year there are numerous deaths as migrants without documents attempt to get to the United States. In the heart of the winter and summer there are frequently deaths from exposure to the elements. Consider a few headlines that demonstrate the perils of illegal border crossing: "Stricken Border-Crosser Found Dead; Another Shot by Mistake" (Associated Press, August 21, 2001); "Train Kills Sleeping Illegal Migrant" (Associated Press, August 23, 2001); "Illegal Entrant Dies in Desert, Fiscal Year 'Deadliest Ever'" (Associated Press, September 26, 2001).

Despite border fences, walls, lights, helicopters, troops, night vision equipment, and radar used to enforce the U.S.-Mexico border, migrants still manage to cross on a daily basis. Indeed, the border crossing process exemplifies migrants' willingness and ability to directly circumvent the laws of one or more nation-states. Obviously, Yucatecans are violating U.S. law by crossing the border without documentation.

Some violate Mexican laws as well; for example, many young men leave Mexico when they reach eighteen even though by law they are expected to remain to serve in the Mexican military. Once migrants reach Dallas they sidestep the legal system of the United States in various ways. In the act of crossing the border, migrants come to see that, although their labor is sought by U.S. employers, they are unwanted outsiders in U.S. society. Immediately, upon arrival, the U.S. legal system becomes something to ignore or circumvent whenever it gets in the way of the pursuit of migrant agendas.

Migrants from Kaal risk their lives coming to the United States to find employment, and to join relatives and friends in Dallas. But most Kaaleños do not come to the United States and stay put. Many travel back and forth to Kaal for religious fiestas and family events. This costs considerable sums of money and involves huge risks, but they do it anyway. Thus, in spite of the structural constraints limiting their choices, migrants have some, however small, degree of agency. James Scott (1985) calls such actions "weapons of the weak." Whether consciously or not, migrants challenge the laws governing the border and, despite the tragic loss of life that occurs, they largely succeed. Migrants pursue their own agendas and life projects and they bravely and cleverly circumvent the militarized border patrol in order to do so. Undocumented migrants are certainly not criminals (implied by the term "illegal alien," which I avoid throughout this book), nor are they hapless victims.

One problem with the current system of immigration is that it creates an arrangement in which access to rewards is dictated by legal status. Thus, native citizens have the most rights, naturalized citizens have most (but not all) of those rights, legal residents have limited rights, and undocumented immigrants have almost none. One hope for the future among the undocumented lies with their children. By law, anyone born on U.S. soil is a U.S. citizen. Thus the U.S.-born children of undocumented immigrants are U.S. citizens. This complicates matters as the second generation has legal and financial rights in the United States that their parents lack. The border crossing is indeed a different experience for the second generation, for they personally do not have to cross surreptitiously. Yet even members of the second generation come to view the border crossing as an ordeal, for their parents, grandparents, siblings, aunts, uncles, cousins, and friends do not have the same privilege of crossing with documentation. One can only imagine the anguish of her four children (only one of whom is U.S.-born) when, after a 1997 flight from Mexico to Dallas, the INS detained Eva. Eva, who is not used to traveling alone, was sent back to Mexico all by herself. Her husband, who has legal residency, flew to Mexico to rescue her and to make arrangements to get her back to Dallas. All the while, Eva's children waited helplessly in Dallas as their mother became an illegal border crosser, risking life and limb to get to the United States.

5

Migrant Agendas and Transnationalism

The lack of economic opportunity in Northern Yucatán and the abundant jobs in Dallas are important conditions for international migration. A more subtle analysis, however, shows how migrants are motivated by other factors as well. Migrant agendas are culturally variable and best studied qualitatively, with ethnographic methods. And there is a transnational dimension involved. As Yucatecan migrants pursue their life projects, they usually end up living their lives across borders. Transnationalism, in other words, results from migrants' attempts to realize their migrant agendas. ⟨

YUCATECAN MIGRANT AGENDAS

Migrant agendas, as I indicated in the introductory chapter, are complex sets of ideas and values that include the goals and motivations for migration, plans in migration, and the coordination of life projects (general life goals) with migration. Among the many aspects of migrant agendas are: orientations to maintaining or severing social ties to both sending and receiving areas, notions of community and citizenship, and settlement plans. Migrant agendas for most Yucatecans in Dallas involve three goals: maintaining the extended family (cf. Lomnitz and Pérez-Lizaur 1984; Warman 1980); preserving cultural and community ties to Kaal; and maximizing social prestige and economic wealth, especially in the context of the sending community. How important each of these goals is to individual migrants varies, of course, according to age and gender, among other factors.

Kaaleños' migrant agendas can be compared to those of other migrant groups in the United States. Other scholars have found kinship to be a central part of migrant goals. Patricia Pessar, for example, writes that the transnationalism of Dominicans in New York results from their desire to maintain ties to kin on the island (1995b). Roger Rouse's (1989) study also emphasizes Mexican migrants' motivation to maintain strong kinship connections to relatives in the homeland. Maintenance of ties of affiliation to the home community has been documented by Robert Smith (1993), who finds, as I do, that Mexican migrants are interested in attending religious fiestas because they are such important community events.

Not surprisingly, motivations having to do with maximizing wealth and prestige have been reported in virtually every ethnographic study of migrants. According to Maxine Margolis, for example, the primary goal of Brazilian migrants in New York is to earn money to make a new life and enhance their status in Brazil (1998:114). In much the same way, Luin Goldring found that the Mexican migrants she studied were concerned with valorizing their status in the context of "Los Animas," their home community (Goldring 1999). Or consider a Portuguese migrant in France who wanted to build a vacation home in Portugal as a way to gain prestige among fellow villagers (Brettell 1982:105). Dominican New Yorkers are also interested in increasing their social status at home. *"Si te va bien, escribe"* (if things go well there, write), go the words of a Dominican song, meaning that if migrants are successful in New York they should write home; if not, they should keep quiet lest they face social embarrassment (Pessar 1995b:14). Obtaining a visa to enter the United States is itself a great source of prestige in the Dominican Republic (Ibid). This is also true among Yucatecans; because it is necessary to prove ownership of wealth in Mexico to obtain a tourist visa, those who get such visas are afforded prestige in the community. In sum, like migrants from other places, the Yucatecans are interested in increasing their social status in Kaal.

In exploring Yucatecan migrant agendas in detail, I describe those aspects that were observable in migrants' behavior and that they felt comfortable talking about in interviews. In Chapter 6, I bring gender into the forefront; the analysis that follows in this chapter is generally applicable to the entire population regardless of gender.

Family

For many Yucatecan migrants (especially women), the extended family, consisting of parents and siblings, has a great influence on their lives. This does not seem to be an adaptation to life in Dallas. Although neolocal residence, in which a couple establishes a new household upon marriage, is common in Kaal, it occurs only when a couple has saved enough money to construct their own house. Upon marriage, a young couple lives with the husband's parents in their home. If the couple does construct their own house it is usually very close—often adjacent—to the home of the husband's parents. (The youngest son is least likely to construct his own house since he usually inherits his parents'.) There is a historical precedent for this pattern. According to ethnohistorical research, extended family households were common in Yucatán throughout the colonial period (Restall 1997:98–109).

Eighty five percent of the migrants I interviewed in Dallas reported sending money to relatives in Yucatán on a regular basis. Monetary remittances are one way that the migrants maintain family connections. Yucatecans send money to spouses and children, but they also send it to parents and siblings. Many reported that they sent money before the fiestas so that their extended family could purchase the clothing and food necessary to celebrate the fiesta in a dignified way. In general, people continue to send money to Yucatán, regardless of how long they have been in the United States.

Another way to maintain family ties is by telephone, something that is made easier by the inexpensive phone cards that are widely available in Dallas. These cards, which can be purchased for five or ten dollars, allow the speaker to talk from half an hour to well over an hour. Sixty eight percent of those interviewed called relatives between once a week and once a month. The most common pattern (30 percent) was every two weeks. In Kaal, many people do not have a telephone in their home so they must depend on those who do. A fee must be paid to relatives who accept calls in their home for the "phoneless," and migrants consider this before calling. The extensive knowledge migrants have about the various long distance calling plans makes clear how important calling Yucatán is. In fact, hardly any migrants—only 3 percent—reported that they "never" called Kaal.

Migrants in Dallas are constantly sharing information about their families in Yucatán with each other. When a person calls Kaal, he or she tells others about the conversation, giving an update of current events, which quickly spreads through the migrant community. Letters, videos, and other mementos are sent home every time someone makes a trip to Yucatán. One example: several weeks before I left to attend fiestas in Yucatán people began to call me to request that I take things to Kaal. I was given letters, photos, videos, clothing, and thousands of dollars to distribute to family members. Migrants called relatives in Kaal to alert them that I was arriving with goods. Within hours of my arrival in Yucatán, people were knocking on the door of the house where I stayed. News travels fast among the Yucatecans in both Dallas and Kaal and between them.

Migrants actively maintain ties of kinship to home despite the difficulties of doing so. Their plans and goals take place in a cultural context in which kinship in the form of the extended family is exceedingly important.

Community Affiliation

Saints and the community-wide fiestas associated with them are of enormous importance throughout the Yucatán peninsula (Elmendorf 1970; Kintz 1990; Press 1975; Re Cruz 1996; Redfield 1941). Throughout the colonial period, the fiesta was crucial in defining the community. According to Nancy Farriss:

> What gave life to the [Mayan] community as a social organism was the shared effort of sustaining their relationship with the saints. The saints did not bestow their benefits gratuitously. One shared in them

only because one had contributed to the collective effort of obtaining them. The cult of the saints was thus more than a mere emblem of group identity. Active participation in the common endeavor gave subjective reality to the territorial boundaries separating one Maya group from another. It also distinguished the Maya from any non-Indians who might share the same territory (1984: 330–31).

As Farris points out, even today the fiestas have a special significance for those who feel part of a Yucatecan community:

> Contemporary Maya sojourners will still make every effort to be on hand for their fiestas, regardless of the cost. I recall the terrible dilemma faced by one worker on an archaeological dig. Should he quit early so that he could attend the week-long celebrations, or stay on and earn more money toward the next year's fiesta, of which he was to be one of the sponsors? He stayed on, as much out of loyalty to the project director as for the extra wages, but a prolonged migraine was the price (1984:332).

Kaal's ritual calendar is important to migrants, who yearn to return "home" for both annual fiestas in May and September, as well as for *carnaval* and the season of Christmas *posadas* (the celebration occurring during and after the birth of Jesus, December 16th-January 6th). In my intensive interviews, all of the twelve men and seven of the eight women intended to visit Kaal within the next two years. Family events like weddings, baptisms, *quinceañeras* (the 15th birthday celebration, symbolizing a coming of age for a young woman in Mexico), and first communions are planned to coincide with fiestas so that migrants can attend family affairs and also participate in the community's festivities. Many go back for these events regardless of how expensive and dangerous the trip may be. Of the 86 survey respondents who had been in the United States for at least two years, over half had visited Yucatán at least once (56 percent). Of the 55 undocumented, almost half (42 percent) had visited at least once. Thus visiting is common and some individuals with immigrant visas visit every year or six months. Several weeks before a fiesta, the Dallas Yucatecan community is abuzz with discussion of airfares to Cancún and Mérida. Several travel agents provide services to the community, and they specialize in getting inexpensive fares at the last minute. One of the most popular is the $99 round-trip charter to Cancún, which is only a four-hour bus ride from Kaal. The problem for undocumented individuals is that they cannot fly back to the United States because they would be required to go through immigration at the airport. For them, going to a fiesta is even more expensive because they have to pay the cost of retaining a *coyote* for the return.

Relations and networks with other Yucatecans in Dallas also reinforce and keep alive ties to Yucatán. As noted, migrants live within walking distance of one another. The men work in restaurants with other Yucatecos in jobs that they found out about from Yucatecan *parientes* (relatives), *compadres* (co-parents), and *compañeros* (friends). They drink together on weekends at a bar directly across the street from the apartment complex where they live and they play soccer every Sunday at a nearby park. Women host parties and religious ceremonies (*novenas*) in their apartments and invite other Yucatecan women. One group of women has "surprise" birthday parties every time one of them has a birthday.

Yucatecos also have rotating credit associations in Dallas, although they are at an early stage of development and are not as well established as the large associations that have been observed among Koreans and other groups in the United States (Light and Bonacich 1988). In the Yucatecan case, several men and women operate what they call *tandas*. People put their name on a list and every two weeks pay $100 per slot. When their number comes up they get the whole pot for that two-week period. This is an effective way to access a large sum of money and pay it off gradually. It is especially important for the undocumented who cannot open bank accounts in the United States without a social security number. One man who runs a *tanda* from his apartment told me how he would never let a non-Yucateco participate because he would not be able to trust him/her. A Yucateco would not be able to get away with not paying because everyone would know about it and (s)he would be ostracized.

Both food and music are ethnic boundary markers (Barth 1969) that symbolize what it means to be "Yucatecan." Yucatecan cuisine requires the use of spices, such as *achiote* and *recado negro*, that are not regularly available in Dallas. Migrants go to much trouble and expense to acquire these items by paying people going to Kaal to bring them back to Dallas. In this way they can eat Yucatecan cuisine in their homes and serve it at parties. Yucatecan food was served at every baby shower, baptism, and first communion that I attended in Dallas. Several individuals have established successful businesses in their homes, preparing Yucatecan food and selling it on weekends. The kind of music preferred by Yucatecans is called *tropical*, and is different from styles found in other regions of Mexico. Mexican migrants from other areas of Mexico favor *norteño* (a regional music originating in Northern Mexico), *tejano* (a derivative of *norteño* that comes from the Texas-Mexico border area), and *banda* (from Sinaloa). *Tropical* is the only style of music that is heard during public dances and private parties in Kaal; it is also the preferred music in Dallas, especially at large gatherings. A preference for *tropical* is a means to show affiliation with other Yucatecos.

Maximization of Prestige and Wealth

In every social setting there are indicators of prestige and these are greatly influenced by cultural factors. In Kaal, prestige is correlated with wealth, but it is also related to an Indian-Mexican continuum that is prevalent throughout Mexico. That is, the further one is culturally from indigenousness, the more prestige one is afforded. In Yucatán there are several indicators of indigenousness. First is language; those who can only speak Maya—and not Spanish—are considered indigenous. Last names that are Maya also yield lower prestige than those that are Spanish. I know of several people who have changed their surname from the Maya word to its Spanish equivalent. Forms of dress are another indicator; women who wear the traditional *huipil* and *rebozo* are more likely to fall on the indigenous end of the continuum. The traditional Mayan house style, wattle and daub walls and thatched roof construction, is generally considered a low status dwelling. Last but not least, phenotypic characteristics such as short stature, straight hair, and dark skin are also associated with indigenousness. People are most likely to drop the outward signs of "Mayanness" when they leave Kaal. For example, before Clara left Kaal for the first time she always wore the *huipil* and *rebozo*. Once she arrived in Dallas she stopped wearing the traditional Yucatecan attire in favor of American-style clothing. Now when she visits Kaal she only wears American clothing, although other migrants pointed out that she used to be a *mestiza;* in other words, she formerly dressed like a Yucatec Maya.

Migration to the United States, as Luin Goldring observes, allows Mexicans to improve their social position in their home communities. In order to cash in on this newly achieved prestige they continue to maintain contact with the community that will validate their new social status and where members "speak the same language of stratification" (Goldring 1999:175).

> Transnational social fields, and places of origin in particular, represent a unique context in which [trans]migrants can make claims to social status and have their status and social capital valorized. This is because the transnational community, like other communities, is a community with a shared version of history and mutually intelligible meanings, particularly concerning status. Individuals and families can improve their houses, wear U.S. clothing styles, drive imported vehicles, buy rounds of drinks, travel to Mexico to get married, return for the patron saint's day, or engage in other practices and know that these claims to mobility, some of which are also claims to community membership, will be properly interpreted. In doing so, they may also reorient the regime of stratification, changing definitions of wealth and poverty, and setting trends in consumption or housing styles (Goldring 1999:189).

In order to increase their prestige in Kaal, migrants visit the Yucatán as frequently as they can and make conspicuous displays of wealth by showering relatives with consumer goods, throwing elaborate parties for family events, acting as *compadres* and sponsoring family affairs of others in Kaal, wearing American-style clothing, and, in the case of men, treating their friends to beer in the cantina. Other displays of wealth can be achieved without ever leaving Dallas. Migrants send money to build well-constructed houses with indoor plumbing, for example, purchase automobiles, or open stores in Yucatán. Migrants can do this because they earn relatively good wages in Dallas compared to Yucatán. Many men in Dallas choose to live in crowded conditions and eat all their meals in restaurants where they work (a benefit of employment) so that they can send money and consumer goods home to their families. A man whose wife is living in a nice house in Kaal is afforded social prestige by other migrants in Dallas, and his wife also profits from more status—and of course the house—in Kaal.

In Dallas, new social distinctions based on legal status and access to social networks (social capital) have emerged among the Yucatecos. León, a twenty-eight-year-old married man, told me how in Kaal his family was considered poor and lacking in social status compared to some other migrants in Dallas. "Here" he explained to me, "we are all the same, so Luis and Armando have to talk to me. In the *pueblo* they never even acknowledged me." This is because in Dallas, León is one of the few migrants to master English, and he has a good job as a cook in a popular restaurant. In the Dallas context he has as much prestige, if not more, than several other men who are from more prestigious families in Kaal. This change in his social position yields prestige in Kaal and when he visits the town he enjoys elevated social status. (Increased prestige in Kaal can lead some non-migrants to feel jealous and competitive with migrants. Some migrants are careful to remain friendly to everyone when they visit Kaal and not to show off, to reduce the risk that their increased prestige will trigger resentment among non-migrants. Those who remain somewhat humble—at least in public—are held in high esteem by the community. Migrants who feel that they can elevate their social position in Kaal are especially likely to limit their primary social contacts to other Yucatecans; maintenance of ties to others with a common history and culture ensures that they are speaking the same "language of stratification" (Goldring 1999). Conversely, several migrants who had high social positions in Kaal and experienced a decline in status in Dallas seem to have expanded their social networks to include non-Yucatecans precisely for this reason.

Most migrants, however, increase their prestige in Kaal as a result of migration and thus are careful to nurture relationships with Yucatecans even when they branch out and form new networks with non-Yucatecans. What is clear is that an important part of migrant agendas of Yucatecos has to do with accumulating economic wealth—and its value is maximized in the context of the community of Kaal.

MIGRANT AGENDAS: TWO EXAMPLES

A close look at the life stories of Luisa Che and Edwin Yeh allow us to see how migrants develop and carry out their plans, strategies, and life projects as they move back and forth between Dallas and Kaal.

Luisa Che

Luisa is thirty-three years old, and is married with two children. Neither she nor her husband Emilio has legal documents or a good chance of legalizing because they arrived in the United States after the IRCA amnesty of 1986. Luisa came to the United States in 1992 to help her sister who had given birth to twins. Eventually she met Emilio, became pregnant, and married him in the downtown Dallas courthouse.

The central part of Luisa's migrant agenda was to show allegiance to her family by helping her sister take care of her infant daughters. She claims that when she first arrived in Dallas she had no plans to remain but hoped to return to Kaal as soon as her nieces were a little older. Her agenda changed because of changing life circumstances. When she became pregnant she knew that she was better off having the child in Dallas. First, she could remain with her husband and also be near her older sister (the mother of the twins) as well as two brothers who had migrated in the meantime. Second, she would have the baby in a hospital (rather than at home as she would have done in Kaal). And, although she did not verbalize this, the fact is that a child born in the United States would be a U.S. citizen. After the birth of her first child, Luisa sent for a younger sister in Kaal who came to Dallas to help her with her new baby. A principal part of Luisa's agenda is still to maintain ties to her family in Kaal. She visited Kaal for the first time in March 1998 and stayed until August. When I interviewed her at her parent's home in Kaal in April she told me that she did not really want to return to Dallas. Her long-term plan, she told me, was to return to live in Dallas long enough to earn enough money to finish building a house in Kaal at which time she would return to Kaal permanently. Whether this will happen is unclear. Indeed Luisa and her husband want their son to attend school in Dallas so that he can learn English and have better opportunities in the future. It may well be that Luisa's agenda will shift with time—and that family ties and other circumstances, including her children's involvement in life in the United States, will keep her in Dallas longer than she now plans.

Luisa's migrant agenda includes:

- maintaining ties to her extended family
- earning money to construct a house in Kaal
- having her son attend school in Dallas so that he can learn English

Edwin Yeh

Edwin is forty years old and arrived in Dallas in 1996. In 1998, when I interviewed him, he was undocumented with no possibility of legalizing his status. Edwin has four daughters, all of whom are in Kaal with his wife Carola. Carola is living in a house adjacent to Edwin's parents' house, fairly close to the central plaza in Kaal. Edwin migrated with his brother, and the two live in the central apartment complex with a married couple from Kaal and their children. Edwin's migrant agenda is straightforward; he wants to earn enough money to complete the construction of his house in Kaal and to fill it with furniture. He also wants money to send his daughters to continue their studies. He lives with a family in Dallas rather than with a group of men from Kaal because that way, he told me, he is less likely to spend a lot of money on alcohol. Because he lives with a family, he is not tempted to drink and stay up late at night. Edwin does not want his wife and daughters to join him in Dallas. Although he had not yet visited his family when I interviewed him, a year later he did go back to Kaal for several months before returning to Dallas to work.

Edwin's migrant agenda includes:

* earning money in Dallas so that he can better his life and the life of his family in Kaal
* maintaining family ties

Both Luisa and Edwin want to earn money so that they can maintain ties to Kaal. Both are motivated by the prospect of having a house in Kaal; the money that they earn in Dallas is seen as a vehicle to prosper in Kaal. But their agendas diverge in that Edwin clearly views Dallas as a place of work only. Luisa has her husband, children, nieces and nephews, and several siblings in Dallas, and her son is in the Dallas school system. Edwin, in contrast, has left his parents and his wife and daughters behind. Members of Edwin's nuclear family, therefore, are active members of the Kaal community and to maintain close ties with them he must maintain participation in the community as well. Of course, a change in Edwin's circumstances could lead to a change in his migrant agenda. If, for example, his wife pressured him to sponsor her migration to Dallas, Edwin's agenda might change accordingly. Although neither Edwin nor Luisa wants to remain in Dallas for the long term, at present there is more of a chance of Luisa settling there than Edwin, since her children are with her and attending Dallas schools.

CIRCUMVENTING THE NATION-STATE

In order to pursue these goals the migrants must circumvent laws in both the United States and Mexico. In Mexico, to take two examples, migrants may avoid military service or attempt to get goods past Mexican Customs without inspection in order to avoid paying tariffs. Far more obvious are the border crossings and the daily acts of noncompliance enacted by the undocumented population in Dallas. To earn money to send to their families in Yucatán, migrants must secure employment without legal documents. There is a trade in false documents in Dallas, where it is possible to purchase social security cards and work authorization permits that will pass inspection by employers. Some migrants make up social security numbers or share the same number with another person. Undocumented migrants who want cars in Dallas engage in other nonlegal strategies. In addition to the trade in social security cards, a flourishing underground market in falsified insurance documentation enables migrants to register their cars. Undocumented migrants in Dallas (and throughout the United States) circumvent immigration law by undertaking fraudulent marriages to U.S. citizens as a way to legalize their status or purchasing phony affidavits or letters to submit to the Immigration Naturalization Service (INS) (cf. Mahler 1995).

Migrant agendas are influenced and shaped not only by economic and political conditions of the global capitalist system but also by culture and local history. What these agendas represent is migrant agency. I am not using agency in a romantic sense that implies that individual migrants have some sort of free will that supersedes or is independent of social structure. Rather, agency means that the values of local culture can be opposed to the nation-state system with its well defined and closely regulated borders. I suggest that the repeated violations of the sanctity of borders, by migrants pursuing their agendas, may ultimately lead to a weakening of the nation-state system. This is important because it shows how the collective actions of local actors can change social structures.

DALLAS–YUCATÁN
TRANSNATIONAL MIGRATION

Because migrant agendas require migrants' involvement in social fields across political boundaries, an examination of migrant agendas inevitably leads to a discussion of transnationalism. Yucatecans in Dallas have in fact established what social scientists call a transnational social field; there is an intense and continuous flow of information, goods, and people between Dallas and Kaal, Yucatán. As Sarah Mahler notes, information and flows of goods—not only body mobility—perpetuate transnationalism (1999:78–79). Among the Salvadoran migrants she studied on Long Island, many could not go back and forth because of the expense and potential danger (many left El Salvador as a result of the civil war and feared return), but they did maintain ties to their homeland through phone calls, letters, and monetary remittances. Yucatecans in Dallas did not have to contend with a civil war back home, but, like the Salvadorans Mahler studied, many were undocumented. Whatever their legal status, Yucatecans continued to send money home. Some maintained economic connections to Kaal even after most members of their extended family migrated to Dallas, since sending money back enhanced their status in Kaal—and offset, at least in part, their low social position in Dallas. Two case studies illustrate how these transnational processes operate in specific instances and the way migrant agendas and transnational connections are closely linked.

"Eva Balam-Ek": A Transnational Woman

Eva is a thirty-four-year-old woman who, when I spoke with her in January 2002, was living in Dallas. Eight of her nine brothers and sisters lived in Kaal and one brother is in Dallas. Eva attended elementary school in Kaal, where she went up to the sixth grade. She married very young, at fourteen. Although her husband, Carlos, had a good job with a chicken processing company in the nearby city of Mérida, in 1983 he decided to go to Dallas to earn more money to build a house, which they have since constructed next to his parents' house. Carlos lived in Dallas but traveled to Kaal for extended six-month periods so that he could witness the birth of his son in 1983 and the baptism of his daughter in 1985. Eva stayed in Kaal in her mother-in law's house and waited for Carlos's visits. Her in-laws, parents, siblings, nieces, and nephews surrounded her so that she had more than adequate social support.

In 1987, Carlos returned to Kaal with the intention of staying permanently. He started his own business, selling chickens and pigs and buying and selling deer skin and leather hides. Eva helped with this enterprise, and they became rather successful until the unforeseeable happened. Carlos had been moonlighting as the driver for a local *Partido Revolucionario Institucional* (PRI) mayoral candidate. (The town is overwhelmingly PRI but there are two competing factions of PRI.) One day Carlos was in a local cantina with the candidate and his entourage and the opposing candidate happened to be there as well. A fight ensued; a man on the opposing candidate's side lost his eye and Carlos was blamed. Carlos felt he had no choice but to flee, since waiting for the police to arrive would only ensure his incarceration. He fled to Dallas shortly after this incident in spring 1991.

This time, Eva did not want her husband to go alone because she was pregnant and her father had just passed away. Her mother and siblings tried to talk her out of going but she refused to listen. She left for Dallas two months later, crossing the border with the help of a *coyote*. Her three children stayed behind with their grandparents. Eva's son joined them in Dallas later that year and her two daughters came the following year even though none of the three had legal status in the United States. Her youngest son was born in Dallas (and is therefore a U.S. citizen). The nuclear family was intact by 1992. Although Carlos is a legal resident, Eva and her three eldest children have no realistic chance of legalizing their status because of legal irregularities in the way that Carlos achieved residency.

Eva's first job in Dallas was as a domestic in Highland Park, a wealthy area within the Dallas city limits. This first job did not work out and she found another job in a Chinese restaurant in downtown Dallas, where she worked for seven months. In 1993 Eva found work with her sister-in-law (Carlos' sister) preparing food at a nearby fast-food restaurant, and she was employed there until she visited Kaal in December 1999. When Eva's niece and nephew's wife migrated to Dallas she was able to get both of them jobs at the fast-food restaurant as well. The fast-food restaurant job afforded Eva considerable freedom to move around in the public sphere of Dallas without her husband, and the money that she earned gave her a sense of accomplishment and satisfaction.

Although she phoned frequently, Eva missed her mother and her siblings. Fortunately, someone in Carlos' family with ties to the American consulate was able to secure tourist visas fairly easily. Carlos' mother Doña Mari and Eva's mother Doña Lupe were able to travel to Dallas regularly on tourist visas and to stay for several months at a time. In fact, when I first met Eva, her mother and mother-in-law were visiting. The women wore *huipiles* and *rebozos,* and their presence in the apartment complex gave it a distinctively Yucatecan flavor. The visits from her mother meant that Eva could stay in Dallas for a long stretch—six years—without going back to Kaal.

In 1997 Eva decided that it was time for a trip to Yucatán. Her husband, a legal resident, had visited several times despite the potential for problems in the town. Once he was able to negotiate a monetary settlement with the man who lost his eye, it was safe for him to visit. September of 1997 was an exciting time because of the yearly fiesta for the patron saint and because of the weddings of two of Carlos' cousins on the weekends bracketing the fiesta. The weekends during and right after a fiesta are difficult times to book an event at the church in Kaal because so many people want to have life-cycle events then. Migrants are always visiting during fiestas so to have an event soon after a fiesta is to ensure that it is well attended.

At the time of her visit in 1997, Eva's four children were all enrolled in Dallas public schools. Because he was born in the United States, and is a U.S. citizen, her youngest child can go back and forth to Mexico without problems. Her other three children are undocumented, so to take them to Kaal and get them back to Dallas would have been difficult and expensive. Eva and Carlos decided to take their youngest with them and leave the other three in Dallas. Eva's brother lives with them in Dallas; it was agreed that he would keep an eye on the three teenagers to make sure they were going to school and behaving themselves.

I happened to go to Kaal at the same time as Eva. Since I stay with her sister, I spent a lot of time with Eva and her husband during their visit. Eva and Carlos slept in their own house despite its unfurnished state. While in Yucatán they went to Mérida to purchase furniture. Eva is very proud of her house; it may have been started with the money remitted by Carlos, but it was finished with her money as well. She was thrilled to furnish it.

Eva participated in many of the fiesta's activities. The first night of the fiesta (the *vaquería*), the symbolic beginning of festivities, is distinctive for the dance held in the plaza. On this one night the women wear their traditional *ternos* (the ceremonial *huipil*) and both men and women dance the *jarana*, the regional dance of Yucatán. Eva wore her *terno* and danced the *jarana* impressively. Not everyone has studied the *jarana* and people respect those who know it. I sat with Eva and her family behind the plaza and we drank beer and talked until four or five in the morning. On each afternoon of the fiesta there are bullfights at 4:00 and there is a dance every night. Eva attended almost all of these events.

I returned to Dallas before Eva did. She had trouble getting back into the United States. Although she had a tourist visa, an INS agent questioned her in the Dallas airport and discovered that she had a job in the United States. She was sent back to Mexico City and had to travel to the border by bus so that she could cross over by foot. She described the stressful train ride to Dallas where INS agents entered the train at various stations and randomly checked documents. She finally made it back to Dallas but she was not eager to go through the crossing ordeal again.

Once back in the normal routine of life in Dallas, however, Eva immediately began to plan her next trip to Kaal. At first she talked about attending the wedding of her sister in April 1998. When that trip was not possible, she began to plan for her 13-year-old daughter's *quinceañera* celebration. Although Eva and Carlos had the *quinceañera* for their older daughter in Dallas, Eva decided that her younger daughter should have her party in Kaal because "*allí se hacen más bonitas las fiestas*" (the parties are better there). She also told me that she wanted her younger daughter to stay in Kaal because she was worried that she was becoming too "Americanized." Her daughter was getting into fights and not doing well in high school. Eva thought that her daughter would learn to become more polite and respectful if she remained in Kaal.

Indeed, in the fall of 1999 the entire nuclear family did go to Kaal together. Eva and Carlos had a *quinceañera* for the youngest daughter and they celebrated Christmas and New Year's Eve in Yucatán. Carlos, Eva, and their eldest daughter then returned to Dallas in January 2000. The daughter who had the *quinceañera* and their two sons remained in Kaal. This family is extended across borders and a transnational orientation is a necessary part of maintaining familial unity.

"José Pérez-Cabrera": A Transnational Man

José is a forty-four-year-old man living in Dallas. He has six siblings, three of whom (brothers) are in Dallas and three (sisters) in Yucatán. José finished the sixth grade and then quit school so that he could help his father in the fields farming his *milpa* and growing and cutting henequen. He later apprenticed as a mason and worked in construction. At the age of eighteen, he got married, and his wife moved in with him in his parents' house. José and his wife had two children, a boy and a girl. When the children were very young, José began working in Cancún, Chetumal, and other faraway places on the Yucatán peninsula doing construction and returning home to visit every one or two weeks. When José found out that his wife was involved with another man while he was away, he petitioned for divorce and won full custody of their two children. His mother, Doña Ana, took primary responsibility for raising them.

José was upset about the divorce, but felt that he now had the freedom to pursue work in the United States, something he had never considered when he was married. In April 1982, José arrived in Dallas for the first time. He came with the help of two other Yucatecan men; they paid his way and helped him get a job right away. He stayed for six years before he went back to visit Kaal. Because he was in the United States during the IRCA amnesty, he was able to obtain legal residency. He struggled to learn English *"para defenderme"* (to defend himself). Although not quite fluent in English when I met him, José knows more English than most other Yucatecans and constantly practices to improve his skills.

After the 1982–1988 stay in Dallas, he began to visit Kaal routinely. Later on, two of his brothers came to Dallas, and the three of them worked in the restaurant business as dishwashers, busboys, and cooks. Once he had legal residency, José decided to sponsor his son (22 years old) and daughter (21 years old). He was successful in getting an immigrant visa for his daughter, but his son missed the age cutoff by several months. (Legal permanent residents can sponsor spouses and minor children.) When I interviewed José both his son and daughter were living with him in Dallas. Since then, his daughter went back to Kaal, got engaged and then married, and returned to Dallas with her husband in October 1999. José's son went back to visit for the wedding but returned to Dallas soon after.

José enjoys working and, even more, having money. In the winter of 2000 he worked two full-time jobs, both cooking positions. Several years ago he decided that he wanted to have a house in Kaal so he saved his money, traveled to Kaal, and bought the materials. He constructed the house himself over the course of several trips. The house sits between the houses of two of his brothers, right next to his parents' home.

José visits Kaal two or three times a year, preferring to go during fiestas, Christmas, and *carnaval*. In September 1999 his daughter was married on the weekend before the fiesta and his sister the following weekend. José, his son, and all three of his brothers traveled to Kaal for the festivities. His parents visit Dallas almost every year during the summer months but, because of the animals that need tending at home, they do not arrive or leave at the same time. His mother, Doña Ana, misses her grandchildren and her sons and so she insists on visiting often (every year) and staying for extended periods (at least a month at a time). Her sons gladly send her money so that she can make the trip.

In May 1999 José's parents visited at the same time so that they could attend the baptism of the newborn son of Jose's younger brother. The baptism was held in Dallas since the baby's father is undocumented and it would have been difficult to have it in Mexico. Also, the mother is from the state of Michoacán, so there was less motivation to have the baptism in Yucatán. José's brother made sure to schedule the baptism for a time when he knew that both of his parents would be in Dallas.

José has been in the United States since 1983 yet his Yucatecan orientation remains strong. He has built and furnished a house, where he stays on his frequent trips to Kaal. When I asked José if he felt that he was still part of the community of Kaal, he responded:

> Yes, I feel like part of the community of Kaal, because I get the urge to go sometimes. I think that I still am part of it since I don't say well, I have my kids here; my parents can visit whenever they want. So there is no problem for me to stay here indefinitely. Do you understand? But no, I still feel like going there. I still want to go there. To see my friends and all that. That's why I still feel like part of the community there.

José emphasized that although his children are with him in Dallas, and his parents visit often, he still feels attached to Kaal.

An attorney suggested that José become a U.S. citizen as a way to help legalize his son's status. Despite the advantages it might bring, José is reluctant to become a U.S. citizen. He understands that he would be able to maintain his Mexican nationality as well, but he still feels uncomfortable about it:

> Well, it's that I don't want to arrive in Mexico or in Yucatán one day and not have any rights there. Do you understand? I would like to have the same rights. To always be Mexican.

So far, José has maintained a transnational kind of life. He went to Kaal in September 1999 for the fiesta of San Miguel and returned to Dallas in October. He made another trip in March 2000 for *carnaval*. His mother and father visited Dallas in the summer of 2000. It is yet to be seen if José will stay in the United States and continue to live a life oriented towards Yucatán or if he will eventually return to live in Kaal on a permanent basis. To date, and for nearly twenty years, he has been part of both places at once, seeking to fulfill his migrant agendas in a transnational arena.

GOODS AND INFORMATION

If many migrants, like José and Eva, maintain a transnational lifestyle, particular goods and information also go back and forth—sustaining transnationalism and allowing Yucatecans to pursue their specific agendas.

Video Recording and Photographs

In some parts of the world, it is impossible to take pictures of people without insulting them or making them angry. This is not a problem among Yucatecans (cf. Koltyk 1998 on the Hmong in Wisconsin). The video recorder is a vital part of their lives. People aspire to purchase one—and those who have video recorders use them often. Cameras and videorecorders are welcome at any event. Because I usually had a camera with me I was often asked to take photos for people and gladly consented.

Photos and videotapes are extremely important to Yucatecans. They collect photos and put them in photo albums and in frames, which they display in their homes. Videotapes of fiestas or life-cycle events are popular commodities in Dallas. For example, Marta is a woman who attended the 1997 September fiesta at the same time as I did. Marta and her husband taped all of what they considered to be the important parts of the fiesta: the *vaquería*, the procession, the bullfight, and the wedding that took place on the Sunday of the fiesta. When they returned to Dallas, people called to ask to borrow the tape. Occasionally, when I went to interview people I had the experience of meeting someone for the first time who told me that he/she saw me dancing in the videotape of that wedding.

The first time I visited Kaal I was introduced to an older couple whose adult children were in Dallas. I was invited into the couple's home and offered the customary *refresco* (soda). As in most houses in Kaal, the main room was rather barren, with only a few wooden chairs. A hammock was hung across the center of the room. As empty as the house was, they did have a TV and a VCR. As we chatted, they asked if I knew their children in Dallas; because it was early in my research I did not and I told this to the couple. "Well, our daughter's son just had a baptism," they said. "Do you want to see the video?" I sat there amazed as I watched a party in Dallas in an apartment that looked familiar, with people I recognized but didn't yet know well. "How can it be?" I thought, "that here I am in Yucatán, Mexico, watching a baptism that took place half a mile from my home in Dallas?"

The tapes of all kinds of events in Dallas are sent back to Kaal. Eva's son and daughter recorded her thirty-second birthday party and that tape was sent to Mexico for viewing. Tapes flow the other way too. In Dallas I was often invited to sit with a group of people who were watching videos of events in Kaal such as *quinceañeras*, weddings, birthday parties, dances, and bullfights. The viewing itself is an experience, and ongoing narrative by the audience reveals much about social norms and social relationships in the Yucatecan Dallas community.

One way I was able to thank people for participating in my research was to give them copies of my photos. When I went to Kaal I brought pictures of migrants in Dallas as gifts and upon my return I gave migrants photos of their relatives in Kaal. Whenever anyone in Dallas has a newly developed roll of film, a group of people inevitably clusters to glimpse the pictures and to make comments and jokes as the photos are passed around.

Yucatecan–Dallas Couriers

People who visit Kaal or those who come to Dallas from Kaal are invariably asked to take goods with them. The most common items to go from Dallas to Yucatán are videotapes, letters, and money, but clothing, electronic equipment, bicy-

Parties in Dallas are videotaped and sent to Kaal.

cles, toys, and CDs are also sent. The Yucatán-to-Dallas route involves goods such as letters, videotapes, food, and medicine. There are two kinds of couriers. First there are people who just happen to be visiting and will take goods for relatives and friends, sometimes for a nominal fee. Second are those few individuals who have established a business going back and forth on a regular basis with the sole intention of taking goods and money to Kaal.

I have already mentioned my own experiences with transnational couriership; every time I went to Mexico or returned to Dallas I was asked to take goods with me. One day, when I was with a group of women in an apartment, the conversation turned to what they would like to take with them to Mexico. As they discussed what they wanted to take—dishes and Tupperware, towels and linens, furniture, and even appliances like refrigerators—I asked why they did not send boxes of their belongings to Mexico by mail. They replied that it was expensive and unsafe; the recipient would have to travel to Mérida to pick up the package and pay for it on that end, and there was the risk that Mexican officials might steal some or all of the contents of a parcel or box. A much better option was to send articles with a person who was going or, better yet, take them yourself when you got the opportunity to go.

People began to prepare for a trip to Mexico weeks in advance by filling enormous boxes with all kinds of goods. When Eva went to Kaal in 1997 half of her apartment was filled with boxes, the huge size of the load related to the fact that it was her first visit after a long absence. In May 1998 I went to the airport with a group of people going to Kaal for the fiesta. Doña Mari (Carlos' mother), who had come to visit Dallas for her granddaughter's first communion, was also heading back to Yucatán in time for the fiesta. We drove to the airport in several cars and trucks, filled to capacity with cargo. Upon arrival at the airport the men, some there merely to help, unloaded and brought the boxes to the airline's ticketing area. Boxes were everywhere. As other passengers approached the line they eyed the cargo curiously. When one of the men finally reached the ticket counter, the other men hurried over to help put the boxes on the scale. The patient ticket agent rejected an absolutely enormous television set, which was barely squeezed into the wrong sized box, covered with towels and tied with rope. (Other ticket agents were not as patient and were clearly annoyed with the extra work that the migrants were causing them). To my surprise, another unwieldy box containing a bicycle was allowed. The Yucatecans knew that they would be charged for the extra boxes, and they pulled out wads of cash to pay the agents. They negotiated and haggled about the weight of several items and argued that each of the several children traveling with them had the right to check two bags. Despite the dirty looks from other passengers and a few angry ticket agents, they were able to get all of their belongings, with the sole exception of the television set, onto the airplane. Their determination and persistence were remarkable.

The several individuals who have established informal courier businesses must deal with airline rules and regulations as well. Doña (Lupe) Ku is a widow of about sixty-five

Doña Lola returns to Kaal with boxes of goods from Dallas.

and a legal resident of the United States; her children live in Dallas and her parents and siblings in Kaal. She and her son have begun to make monthly trips to Kaal, bringing goods for a fee. They also charge $5 for every $100 that they take to Yucatán; they bring the money directly to the recipient and pay in American dollars. Money couriers guarantee their service; if they lose the money or are robbed they are still responsible for seeing that the money is paid. This is a bargain since sending money via Western Union, Money Gram, or any of the other local money transfer companies is more expensive, and money is paid out in pesos rather than dollars. (In fact, just recently a class action suit has been filed against Western Union and Money Gram because of deceptive practices whereby they misrepresented the value of the peso and profited from the difference between what the Mexican bank was paying the company and what they were giving to the money transfer recipients in Mexico.) On the return trip, Doña Ku brings back Yucatecan spices and other foodstuffs that are not available in Dallas and she sells these as well.

Another woman, from a Yucatecan town near the ruins of Uxmal, is a friend of some of the Dallas Yucatecans from Kaal. She is constructing a house in Mérida and travels there from Dallas with her husband once a month to work on it. She, too, brings back Yucatecan delicacies such as *achiote* (a red spice used on chicken or pork), *pepita* (ground pumpkin or squash seeds), and *Xtabentun* (a liquor made from anise), and sells them to other Yucatecos.

In sum, Doña Ku and her son, like other couriers, provide a much-needed service that Yucatecans in Dallas are willing to pay for. As long as people travel back and forth between Yucatán and Dallas there will be an associated transfer of goods as well. For the Yucatecans, traveling light is a contradiction in terms.

House Construction

Another part of the transnational social field is house construction, which demonstrates a strong and continued orientation to Yucatán among migrants in Dallas (cf. Brettell 1979). Eight of the nine couples that I interviewed in depth either had built or were in the process of building houses in Yucatán. The husband of the ninth couple, the youngest son in a well-off family, will inherit his parents' house, which is why he has not bothered to build his own.

One of the nine couples who are paying off a mortgage in Dallas said that they have a house in Kaal so that they can stay there when they visit for fiestas. Another couple explained that once the house was completed the wife will return to Mexico with their children, and the husband will live in the United States for extended periods of time so that he can remit money to them. Two couples have houses in Mérida, which they plan to return to at some unspecified time in the future. One of the two couples also owns a house in Dallas. Even when people buy a house in the United States they do not lose their orientation to, or involvement in, life in Yucatán.

Yucatecan and Mexican Spaces

Various businesses and public venues in Dallas are "transnational spaces" where migrants can buy products from home and experience a Yucatecan atmosphere deep in the heart of Texas. Mexicans all over the United States take public spaces and make them their own, something recognized by scholars writing about the Latinization of the United States (Gutierrez 1998). The Spanish print media and television have expanded exponentially in recent years, and Mexican popular culture has changed the cultural landscape especially in the southwestern United States (Gutierrez 1998:315–317).

My first contact with Yucatecans in Dallas was with Alfredo, who established a restaurant in his apartment. Alfredo and his wife Luz prepared Yucatecan delicacies in their home every weekend. They set up a long table with condiments and napkins where people could eat. Alfredo's refrigerator was stocked with beer and sodas that he sold along with food. Part of the charm of Alfredo's place was Alfredo himself who loves to talk and has a wicked sense of humor. Often, he sat at the table drinking beer and talking with clients while Luz did all of the work in the kitchen. On weekends, the apartment had the atmosphere of a business establishment. There was a constant flow of people, some eating and others picking up food to bring back to their homes. The phone was constantly ringing as people phoned in orders.

This was clearly a Yucatecan space in Dallas. Almost all of the clients were Yucatecos (even though not all were from

Kaal) and the conversation was oriented towards Yucatán. The food was the cuisine of Yucatán and none other. A Yucatecan flag hung on the wall alongside an enormous sign that proclaimed *"se vende tarjetas de teléfono aqui"* (phone cards for sale here). Alfredo and Luz's business enterprise was successful for years but, unfortunately, when the apartment management changed, Alfredo and Luz were prohibited from selling food.

Doña Nora, a woman over sixty with twin adult sons in Dallas, also runs an informal business there. A true transnational entrepreneur, she also runs a *puesto* (stand) at the market in Kaal where she sells food. She operates the restaurant in Dallas out of her sons' apartment on her extended visits there. Her business was initially not quite as successful as Alfredo's, but once he stopped preparing food, it thrived. When she is in Dallas, Doña Nora prepares Yucatecan dishes, which she sells each and every weekend. Her "restaurant" is a place where Yucatecos come not only to eat but also to socialize with other Yucatecos.

Flea markets (*pulgas*) are another transnational space. The *pulga* in Grand Prairie, Texas, is only about 15 miles from the center city of Dallas. The overwhelming majority of both vendors and buyers are Latino, and Spanish is the language of choice. The goods are a mix of Mexican and American, but all items are oriented towards Latino consumers. Writing of the *pulga* in Austin, Texas, Ricardo Ainslie calls it the "quintessential potential space for Mexican immigrants," likening it to the bustling *zócolos* which are such a central part of the towns they have left behind (1998:290).

Yucatecans—who identify as Mexicans as well as Yucatecos—also participate in more inclusive "Mexican spaces" in some social contexts. In predominantly White, English-speaking Dallas they view themselves and are seen by others as *Mexicanos*, and, in fact, they are relatively comfortable patronizing stores and businesses that cater to a broad Spanish-speaking, Latino clientele. On shopping ventures with Yucatecan women, we went to branches of Target and Payless Shoes where the majority of customers and employees were Spanish-speaking. A mall of choice is in Oak Cliff, an area of Dallas with a long history of Latino and African-American residential concentration. The two supermarkets of choice

(Danal's and Carnaval) are both oriented to a Latino market. Fresh *tortillas* and *masa* for *tamales* are regularly available, as are countless varieties of chili peppers and other Mexican produce. Many Yucatecan men and some women enjoy dancing, and Dallas has several popular Latino nightclubs. When I attended one such establishment with a group of Yucatecan women I was one of the only non-Latinos in the establishment; English was not spoken.

Still, in more localized relations, Yucatecans identify with others from Yucatán and distinguish themselves from other, non-Yucatecan Mexicans. This is why local establishments such as Alfredo's and Doña Nora's are so successful. Attending Yucatecan parties is another way to create a Yucatecan space. The food, music, and conversation at such parties are all focused on Yucatán. Clearly, there is a strong desire to recreate Yucatecan social space in a city dominated by Mexicanos from other parts of Mexico like Guanajuato and Zacatecas.

Local Job Markets

According to Sassen, local labor markets may be transterritorial and can even transcend borders (Sassen 1995:111) as word-of-mouth recruitment operates in more than one national arena. Local labor markets in Dallas, at least those segments where Latino immigrants represent a large proportion of the workforce, have become transnational in this way. Almost all of the Yucatecan men work in restaurants where the majority of kitchen workers are Yucatecan, and recruitment processes operate across the U.S.-Mexico divide.

Consider Marcelo's restaurant. In the early 1980s, Marcelo, an Italian immigrant, found sponsors for his restaurant venture and opened an upscale restaurant close to where Yucatecans live. Before becoming a restaurateur, Marcelo waited tables at a hotel where several Yucatecos worked and he befriended a few of them. When Marcelo opened the restaurant in 1984, he hired Yucatecos for key kitchen positions regardless of whether or not they had legal work authorization. The restaurant thrived and Marcelo was pleased with the way the Yucatecos worked. As his business expanded, he was able to recruit other Yucatecans by asking current employees for recommendations. In 1984 few Yucatecos lived in Dallas and almost all worked at Marcelo's. Once Marcelo had hired all of the possible Yucatecan men in Dallas he began to encourage his Yucatecan workers to recruit relatives and friends in Kaal. He also needed replacements when, as sometimes happened, Yucatecos had disagreements with him and quit.

Over the years, Marcelo's business went through ups and downs. Some of his Yucatecan employees became frustrated that their paychecks could not always be cashed, because of insufficient funds in the restaurant's bank account, and they left to find other jobs. But Marcelo always had a core group of about five loyal Yucatecan workers who stayed with the restaurant during hard times. This core group was Marcelo's key to untapped labor in Kaal. Indeed, he recruited labor by allocating money to his core employees who used it to help pay the costs of border crossing for new employees. These new migrants were then indebted to their Yucatecan sponsors and obligated to work in the restaurant until their debts were settled. Marcelo's preference for Yucatecan workers led to the development of a transterritorial local labor market in which non-migrants in Kaal came to understand that if they migrated to Dallas there was a restaurant where they were almost guaranteed employment.

Undoubtedly, further study would reveal similar transterritorial employment networks that link specific restaurants and hotels in Dallas to specific towns and villages in other parts of Mexico. Nor is this process unique to Dallas; it can be found in other places where there are labor niches in which migrants predominate, chain migration is prevalent, and the demand for labor is high (see Hagan 1994 for Guatemalan Maya in Houston).

CONCLUSION

The transnational social field I have described in this chapter includes kinship connections, community ties, networks of friendship and association, and employment markets that bridge two localities: a neighborhood in Dallas, Texas, and

Kaal, Yucatán. These transnational ties are maintained through body mobility of migrants as well as through the movement of goods and information across borders. A central theme throughout this book is that transnationalism is created through the actions of migrants—actions that are inspired by their migrant agendas. Transnationalism represents agency in the migration process because it embodies how migrants actively maintain cross-border social ties that they find important and how they circumvent the nation-state system to do so.

6

Women and Men Migrants

This chapter examines how gender influences the migration experience. It is clear that Yucatecan men and women in Dallas operate in distinctive social spheres and that their daily lives differ in many ways. This is not, I suggest, solely an adaptation to migration. In Kaal as well as in Dallas, men and women live a gendered existence that dictates the kind of work they do, the places they go, and the appropriate activities they undertake. To understand the role of gender in Dallas, then, it is necessary to also understand the Kaal context.

In studying male and female migrant agendas, I was surprised to find more similarities between spouses than the literature suggests. As Patricia Pessar (1995a) points out, feminist scholars often approach their data with preconceived notions about what they expect to find, and this can lead to oversimplification and misrepresentation. Indeed, I had expected that because of Yucatecan women's increased access to the public domain in Dallas, they would want to remain in the United States (see Grasmuck and Pessar 1991; Hondagneu-Sotelo 1994) but this was not the case. I found that women were more likely than men to consider permanent return to Mexico and that men more commonly intended to stay in the United States in the long term. To deal with this issue, it is helpful to investigate the gendering of social life along several dimensions.

Women and Men from Kaal: Gendered Social Spheres

To compare the lives of men and women in Dallas, and to explore how migrant agendas might diverge along gender lines, I conducted a series of in-depth interviews with nine migrant women, all married or in consensual unions, as well as with their husbands. I also interviewed two non-migrant women in Kaal and their husbands in Dallas, and was able to draw on my larger sample of one hundred migrants for insights into gender differences.

Despite the consensus that I found between Yucatecan migrant spouses in their household goals, gender conflicts arise both within marriage and in general. For example, men who refuse to provide for their families are viewed with contempt by women and men alike. And there are such men, even among migrants with wives in Dallas. A few men act as if they are breadwinners, with all of the rights to be in charge of (*mandar*) their families, but are not employed even though they could readily find work. Their wives' employment enables them to drink heavily in the evening and forfeit work the following day. Inevitably they are fired and must find new jobs. Other Yucatecans talk about such men behind their backs and call them lazy (*"no le gusta trabajar"*), irresponsible (*"es muy irresponsable"*), and/or alcoholic (*"puro toma hace"*). These are extreme cases. Yet as long as men contribute money for beer, they do not lack male Yucatecan drinking partners. On the whole, couples have common agendas, which are negotiated and renegotiated over time. At the same time, men and women experience Dallas differently and operate, in many ways, in separate social spheres. This is particularly evident in regard to employment, the public vs. domestic spheres, leisure, and transnationalism.

Employment

Married women in Kaal are usually not employed outside the home—they are housewives. Once Yucatecan women arrive in Dallas, however, the taboo against female employment disappears and they search for jobs, principally as domestic workers. Despite their desire to find jobs, Yucatecan women have low rates of employment relative to men in Dallas. Also, as among other migrant groups where women tend to cluster in domestic employment, men and women have different working environments (Hagan 1998; Hondagneu-Sotelo 1994). Since many men work in restaurants with fellow Yucatecans, they socialize after work. All of the Yucatecan men have similar work schedules, which means that they have their time off at the same time. Much to the chagrin of their wives, this affords men the constant opportunity to visit and drink with other men. Indeed there is a conflict between men and women over how much time a man should spend *en casa* with his wife versus in the *calle* with his friends.

Women domestics, by contrast, usually do not work with others and most women in other jobs do not have Yucatecan coworkers. Women usually travel to and from work by bus, and tend to go to work alone. Once on the job, domestics have no contact with other people apart from the family who owns the home and other household workers, if there are any. Since they generally use the same bus routes at the same hours each day, women often get to know other women on the bus. Several women mentioned conversations that they had with other Latinas on the bus, and one found a domestic job by pursuing a contact given to her by a fellow Latina bus passenger. A few women work preparing food in fast-food establishments; a group of four related Yucatecan women are employed at one such place within walking distance of the apartment complex. Another woman also works preparing food at the same fast-food restaurant that employs her son.

Another important difference between men's and women's work is the relative ease of finding jobs. Men have a much easier time locating employment because restaurant work is abundant and because Yucatecan friendship and family networks lead them directly to jobs. A man can readily find a new job by asking Yucatecan friends and family if there are openings in their places of employment. When a new restaurant opens, men travel in a group to apply for a position there.

Although there is demand for domestic employment in Dallas, domestic work is more difficult to find than the men's restaurant jobs (cf. Hagan 1998). It is not that the job market is saturated; a glance at the lengthy domestic employment section of the newspaper suggests otherwise. The fact is, though, that Yucatecan women refuse to take live-in domestic jobs, preferring instead to work a fixed number of hours and return to their own homes. This limits their choices because many employers are looking for live-in workers. Also, employers do not like to hire women unless they have been referred by people whom they know and trust. Employers expose their homes (and sometimes their children) to domestic workers and are careful to select people who are reliable and trustworthy. Since most domestic work is informal there are no protections for either worker or employer. Relying on information and references from people they know mediates uncertainty for both. Women looking for domestic positions ask their friends but rarely find jobs this way. The best way to find domestic employment is from a current employer, something that is impossible for the unemployed. When a Yucatecan woman is cleaning a house one or two days a week and hears that a friend of her boss needs a domestic employee, she is most likely to take that work herself. This is valuable information and if she does not want the extra work she will tell a relative or a close friend. One woman held a domestic position that required her to work almost every day. She complained that she was overworked, underpaid, and treated disrespectfully by the employer's daughter. She finally grew tired of this situation and quit. By quitting, however, she lost her ability to rely on that employer as a job reference. As a result, she was unable to find domestic employment and briefly worked at several other jobs (in a dry cleaning business and factory work), none of which she liked enough to keep. She remained unemployed for months and constantly asked her friends (and me) about other domestic employment. She was not successful in finding another domestic position.

The difficulty that women have in finding domestic employment and the relative abundance of restaurant work leads to a puzzling question: why don't women get jobs at restaurants? One reason is that the workforce is gendered, and most of the most highly valued jobs in upscale restaurants (chefs, cooks, and waiters) are considered men's jobs by those doing the hiring (Cheng 1999). Still, demand for restaurant labor is high and there is no apparent reason why a kitchen manager would prefer to hire men for jobs such as dishwasher or table busser (indeed women sometimes hold these positions). I suggest that the gendered structure of the workforce combined with cultural constraints within the migrant community prevent women from entering the restaurant labor niche. Men work in upscale restaurants as dishwashers, bussers, and food preparers where most of their co-workers are men—and men do not want their wives in an all-male or mostly-male workplace. In contrast, domestic employment is considered gender appropriate because women are isolated and not working in the presence of other men. Most Yucatecan men jealously protect their wives and many do not want them working near other men. Women know how their husbands feel about this, and may themselves feel uncomfortable working with other men, so they do not pursue restaurant employment. Also, men do not want their wives in their own workplaces because it would limit their own freedom on the job. Given the flexibility in mens' working hours, women never know exactly when their husbands leave work. Men take advantage of this by drinking with their friends for a few hours and then reporting to their wives that they were working late. It is notable that most of the women working in fast-food restaurants are doing so in the company of other Yucatecan women. Also, the few women who have temporary jobs bussing tables at banquets also work with a group of women (in one case three sisters work together). Perhaps those jobs are considered appropriate because the women work together with other Yucatecan women and, therefore, the eyes of the community are always upon them. None of the Yucatecan women works in an upscale restaurant where Yucatecan men are employed.

Casa y Calle (Household and Public Spheres)

In Kaal, and to some extent throughout rural Mexico, there is an important gendered distinction between the *casa* (the home) and the *calle* (the street). In ideal terms this means that women are confined to the domestic sphere. "Decent" women spend most of their time in their homes—if they leave the house they are usually accompanied by kinsmen. If women do venture off alone, they are careful to let someone know—whether it be their husbands or in-laws—exactly where they will be at all times. When women go out, it is only to run errands for their households or to visit inside the *casas* of family or friends. It is appropriate for men, on the other hand, to be in the *calle*. When men are in the *calle* it means that they are "out"—and their wives and mothers usually do not know where they are. Men in Kaal, therefore, have more freedom in the *calle* than do women. Whereas men can come and go as they please, women cannot.

This changes in Dallas because there, men's undocumented legal status severely curtails their freedom in the public sphere. From a male perspective, in Dallas the *calle* is more restricted than it is in Kaal; it is not the exclusive domain of men and the danger of detention by the INS is ever present. From the female point of view, despite the risks of apprehension by immigration officials, living in Dallas provides an opportunity to gain access to the *calle* that they did not have in Kaal.

The *casa–calle* distinction in Dallas is also transformed because of the new employment situation faced by migrants. In Dallas, most Yucatecan women anticipate that they will work outside the home, whereas in Kaal married women expect to remain *en casa*. Furthermore, men in Kaal prefer to maintain the breadwinner role and discourage or prohibit their wives' employment. Yet in Dallas, economic necessity requires women's participation in the labor force (cf. Pessar 1995b on Dominicans in New York). Wage work increases women's ability to navigate the public sphere and allows them to develop and maintain their own networks of social exchange apart from their husbands' networks. It is important to remember, however, that around a third of the Yucatecan women in Dallas are unemployed and these women are unable to form such networks. But for most Yucatecans in Dallas, as opposed to in Kaal, staying home—and not working—is not seen as desirable by either women or men. It is a result of limited opportunities in the labor market, not a cultural prohibition against female employment.

How are relations within the *casa* transformed in the Dallas context? Some scholars have found that as migrant women participate in the labor force, husbands become more likely to help out around the house with chores (Foner 1978; Guendelman and Perez-Itriago 1987). Cecilia Menjívar's study of Salvadoran and Guatemalan indigenous and Ladina (culturally non-indigenous) women in California suggests that this can be culturally variable; indigenous Guatemalan couples had more egalitarian gender relations than Ladino Salvadorans and Guatemalans (Menjívar 1999:610). What I found was that among Dallas Yucatecans, women's employment did nothing to reduce their burden of household caretaking duties (see Goldring 1996; Min 1998).

In Kaal, most women are responsible for almost all cooking, laundering, food shopping, house cleaning, and childcare. Women in Dallas, whether or not they are employed, are also responsible for these tasks. In Dallas, however, women are more likely than in Kaal to experience a double day because women in Kaal are less likely to be employed outside the home. This burden is even more onerous when women live in apartments occupied by people beyond the nuclear family. It is common for a married couple and their children to share an apartment with brothers-in-law, adult siblings, *compadres,* or friends of either husband or wife. Lena, for example, lives with her husband and three children, her husband's brother and brother in-law (the husband of his sister), and two men who are friends of the family. Lena is responsible for all the cooking; the visiting men contribute to the rent and reimburse her for the extra expenses for food. Lena works full time at a fast-food restaurant and must purchase and prepare food in the afternoons when she returns from work.

Even though men are working in restaurants, where they learn how to wash dishes, clear tables, and cook, they do not perform these tasks at home if they live with their wives. Some women told me that their husbands sometimes prepared special dishes or brought home leftovers from the restaurants where they work, but that these were not common occurrences. Women say that they do not like the food that men prepare (pasta, continental cuisine) and prefer to eat Mexican dishes. Men claim that they do not know how to prepare Mexican food, thereby ensuring that women will remain in the kitchen. When men live in male-only apartments, they must perform all of their own household tasks. Indeed, I observed men in these apartments cooking (Mexican food), mopping the floors, returning from trips to the grocery store, and doing their own laundry. Yet the moment that the men's spouses join them, women take over all of these tasks.

In conclusion, some of the gendered relations within the *casa* and *calle* are transformed in the Dallas context. For employed women, there is a new freedom to be in the *calle* that they did not have in Kaal. Yet this does not lead to much change in the domestic sphere—women in Dallas are still responsible for all housekeeping duties.

Leisure

Men and women participate in some leisure activities together. Both attend life cycle events such as *quinceañeras,* first communions, and baptisms. Spouses arrive at the same time but once there, men and women usually self-segregate. Men congregate in one area, usually outside, and drink beer; women, often with children in tow, sit together and talk, also drinking beer but in substantially lower quantities than the men. Generally, the only exception to this gender segregation occurs when there is dancing because men and women dance with each other.

On the whole, leisure activities are highly gendered, and most gatherings are clearly female or male. Baby showers and women's birthday parties are usually women (and children) -only events. Children's birthday parties are often, but not always, female-only gatherings. Men gather together to watch sporting events, play soccer, drink, and gamble.

Surprise birthday parties are regular women's events that have special meaning to them. Since almost all men work on Friday and Saturday nights, these are times when women gather with other women. Most women in the apartment complex are friends and when one has a birthday the others throw her a surprise party. Of course the regularity of these events precludes any real surprise, but all involved behave as if it is so. On the evening of the party the women gather in one apartment, each bringing a dish that she has prepared or bought and an inexpensive gift. Together all of the women walk to the birthday celebrant's apartment, knock on the door and, when it is opened, yell *"sorpresa!"* (surprise). The celebrant feigns surprise, all enter the apartment, and the party commences. For the next several hours the women eat, drink beer (and sometimes rum), and dance. These parties are opportunities for women to relax, have fun, and behave in ways that would make them uncomfortable in mixed gender company. Women dance arm in arm with each other, joke about sex, and generally behave in a rowdy way. I recall one woman taking a plastic tube and putting it to her groin as if it were her penis and mimicking (and mocking) mens' sexuality. The others found this to be hilarious. The women make fun of men in other ways, usually by mimicking mens' behavior while dancing or drinking. These parties usually last until around midnight, which is the hour that husbands begin to arrive from work.

As for men, on Saturday and Sunday nights, many gather together for all-night drinking binges. There is a bar close to the apartment complex, and men go there after work until the legal hour to sell alcohol passes. They then head to the apartment complex parking lot to drink beer until it is all consumed. Women are not pleased by this behavior and, as best they can, try to prevent their husbands from participating. But men are pressured by other men to drink and to defy their wives. If a man continually refuses drinking invitations from fellow Yucatecos, he is labeled *"mandilón"* (controlled by his wife) and becomes the victim of teasing. One woman explained how groups of men often taunt a man they perceive as *mandilón* until he arrives home drunk, angry, and ready to beat up his wife. People reported that domestic violence was fairly common and almost always occurred when the husband was drunk. Sober men are afraid to hit their wives because they know that women and children can call the police and have them arrested, a pattern observed among Vietnamese (Kibria 1993:121–125) and Jamaican migrants as well (Foner 1997:971). Several Yucatecan women have reported their husbands to the authorities and the men were sent to jail. Interestingly, they did this despite the apparent danger in bringing attention to themselves since many of these women were undocumented and the men legal residents. No doubt, the women were encouraged by the fact that the Dallas police and Latino media have actively campaigned against domestic violence and urged women to call the police if they are in danger, whether or not they have legal documentation.

On Saturdays and Sundays women like to go shopping and, if their husbands are home and not terribly hung over from a drinking binge the night before, they will go together as a family. If not, the women often go shopping with other women. There are several discount stores where women like to shop and they can get there by foot or by bus. Anyone with a car is asked to take people shopping, and on weekends people pile into cars to go to stores that are not easily reached by bus.

For the most part, men and women have different friendship networks. Men who prefer to spend a lot of time with their wives and children are constantly pressured by other men to leave their wives at home and congregate with other men during leisure hours. This peer pressure is intense. Several men, who had quit drinking, told me how difficult it was to maintain friendships with Yucatecos if they did not drink with them. Other Yucatecos were suspicious of, and refused to socialize with, them because they did not drink. Women do not pressure each other to drink; in fact they scorn anyone who drinks too much, which in Dallas is defined as more than one or two beers, especially if there is no food. In Kaal, drinking is more socially acceptable for women than in Dallas.

Transnationalism

Both men and women seek to maintain ties to friends and family in Kaal. Both telephone, send letters, and remit money to relatives. Both men and women also speak of their *pueblo* with nostalgia and longing. Yet it is easier and more common for men (both with and without papers) to visit Kaal. Partly this is because men are less vulnerable to violence than women, and are thus more willing to risk crossing the border without legal documentation. Women with legal documentation can visit without legal problems as long as they have money to do so, and several women do visit frequently. Although many women without legal documentation cross over too, it is commonly agreed, by both women and men, that it is a more dangerous proposition for women to cross the border surreptitiously. The real risks of being sexually assaulted, robbed, kidnapped, or murdered at the border prevent all but the most courageous women from attempting an illegal border crossing. When women do visit Kaal, child-care arrangements enter into their plans in a way that they usually do not for men. For example, during an interview session, a Yucatecan woman pointed to a calendar and described her summer vacation plans. She would leave Dallas with her young son in an airplane. They would return a month later, allowing a week of cushion time at the border so that they would be back in Dallas in time for the child's first day of school. When men go to Mexico, especially if their wives are there, they basically stay until their money runs out.

Although couples in Kaal live with the husband's parents upon marriage, women in Kaal want houses of their own. Many of the women who migrate to Dallas are doing so to save the funds necessary to construct their own houses in Kaal. These women talk about plans to return to Kaal once their homes are completed. They accept the likely possibility that men may have to stay in Dallas in order to remit money.

And there is another element involved in male–female transnational ties and orientations. Given Yucatecan women's limited employment options and that unemployed women do not develop the strong work-related social networks found among Yucatecan men, women in Dallas tend to feel more isolated and bound to the Yucatecan community. Also, as mentioned before, employed women find themselves working a double day as housework remains solely their responsibility. This may help explain why Yucatecan women migrants lack the strong settlement intentions that are so prevalent among women in other U.S. migrant populations.

CASE STUDIES OF MIGRANT COUPLES

An analysis of particular life histories and migrant agendas of husbands and wives sheds light on the specific ways that men and women come to negotiate their goals—and the similarities and differences in their experiences and plans. The following four case studies represent people with different legal statuses—a critically important distinction for Yucatecans.

An Undocumented Pair:
Juan and Lupe

Juan (35 years old) and Lupe (31 years old) are originally from Kaal. Juan's now-deceased father was a successful merchant who bought produce, livestock, wood, and other goods directly from *campesinos* (peasant farmers) so that he could sell them for profit. He had a ranch nearby, left to him by his grandparents. Probably because of his financial success, Juan's father had six "wives," although he was only legally married to one of them. A result of this quasi-polygynous situation is that Juan has nineteen brothers and sisters, some significantly older than he is. When Juan was only eight years old his father passed away and some of his older siblings quickly managed to obtain all of their father's land holdings. Knowing that he could not rely on his family for employment, when Juan finished *secundaria* at the age of thirteen, he went to Cancún to study for a technical career in the hotel industry. He stayed with brothers in Cancún and eventually dropped out of *técnico* (technical school) so that he could work. He worked at several different jobs until he became a cab driver in 1982. He had been working as a taxi driver for fifteen years when he decided to go to the United States.

Lupe also relocated to Cancún when she was thirteen. Her father was a *campesino* in Kaal and her mother migrated daily to Mérida where she worked as a domestic servant. Lupe quit school after the third grade so that she could work to help her parents and allow her younger siblings to continue their studies. The combined income was still insufficient and the family felt it necessary to go to Cancún in 1980 in search of better economic opportunities. Although Lupe had been forced to terminate her studies in Kaal, in Cancún she earned enough money to study to become a beauty stylist and a seamstress. With these new skills she began making and selling clothing. With the money she earned she traveled to Mérida and purchased more clothing, which she brought back to Cancún to sell for a profit. She ran this business until she got married to Juan in 1985, at which time she gave the business to her mother who has continued it to this day.

Juan and Lupe met in Kaal but began dating in Cancún. They decided to marry in Cancún, and many people from Kaal traveled there to attend the wedding. After their wedding they lived in an apartment for three years and saved their money. They bought a plot of land in Cancún and constructed their house over the course of seven years. The house is now unoccupied but Lupe's parents watch it for them while the couple is in Dallas. Even when both Juan and Lupe lived in Cancún, they maintained constant contact with friends and relatives in Kaal and in Dallas. Both continued to be involved in the ritual life of Kaal, although Lupe seems to have been more attached than Juan; she talked about how she attended each and every fiesta, arriving before it began and remaining well after it was over. Juan, on the other hand, only went to Kaal for short visits and returned to Cancún right away. Juan and Lupe have an adopted daughter who was born in 1993, seven years after they married.

Juan came to Dallas for the first time in December 1997. Lupe wanted to go with him but he would not let her, claiming that it was too expensive. He told her to stay and work in Cancún for at least six months so that she could save enough money to pay her own way to Dallas. Less than two weeks after his arrival in Dallas he called and said that a friend was willing to loan him the money so that she and their young daughter could join him in Dallas. Thrilled and at the same time sad to leave her parents behind, Lupe prepared for the journey. Mother and daughter flew to the border and crossed over with the help of a *coyote* arranged by her husband. They arrived just in time for Christmas, and became part of the Kaal community in Dallas.

When I asked why he came to the United States, Juan told me, "to experience the American way of life." In emphasizing the desire for adventure and travel, rather than pure economic necessity, Juan was elevating himself above the rest of the group, which is undoubtedly related to his father's position as a relatively wealthy merchant in Kaal rather than a *campesino* like the parents of most migrants in Dallas. When I asked about his plans, he first told me that he wanted to return to Cancún that following December. Other Yucatecans, he claimed, wanted to stay in the United States for longer because, unlike him, they had no real prospects for economic success in Yucatán:

> Most stay because they have found a lifestyle, because of all the time they have here they are more established here. On the other hand, my situation is that I have more options to find a better job and advance. They came here because of the [economic] situation in Kaal. They don't have the same facilities available that I do to have a business or something [in Mexico].

Lupe has a somewhat different agenda—saying she wants to stay in Dallas for a longer period of time, for at least two years. Her two sisters came to Dallas two years prior to her own arrival; she had wanted to come to the United States for a long time to visit them. Now that she is in the U.S., she wants to work hard and earn money so that she can return to Cancún and expand the business that she started so long ago. She also wants to keep her daughter in school so that she can learn English and have a useful job skill in Mexico. Over the course of several interviews, Juan and Lupe reported about their negotiation and compromise over this issue of return. At first Juan told me that he was going to return to Cancún without Lupe because, as his wife, she has the right to make her own decisions:

> Well, she has to decide because it's not like they say that because I am married to her that I can tell her what to do. She has to think about it. She has to put her feet on the ground and think about her decision. She can decide. Just because we are married, I don't want to say that she has to do what I think. She has her own opinion and I accept it.

Later Lupe told me that she had convinced Juan to stay with her in Dallas:

> I told him if he wanted to go that he should go but that I wasn't going. But now he says he is going to

wait for me. In other words, now his plans are the same as mine. The plan is to stay two more years and then leave together without returning. Because his plan was to leave before me. But I told him no, because our daughter is in school. I wanted to take advantage of her studies. He did not see it my way before, but now he does. He said that he would stay.

One part of Juan's migrant agenda is to foster networks with non-Yucatecans. Juan, in fact, indicated that he has friends from places besides Yucatán such as Guanajuato, Monterey, and Acapulco. Lupe and Juan do not live in the central apartment complex, but within walking distance, and other Yucatecos live in their complex too. Although Juan criticizes his fellow Yucatecos for being irresponsible with their jobs, drinking too much, and being envious of each other, he still lives and works among Yucatecos. Lupe is less critical of the other Yucatecos and maintains constant close contact with them.

Juan, Lupe, and their daughter are all undocumented with no possibility of legalizing under current immigration law. This has some influence on their ability to make long-term plans in the United States. At this point their daughter is in elementary school, and both parents expressed an interest in keeping her there at least until she masters English. Yet neither Juan nor Lupe has intentions to settle in the United States. Both are focused on Yucatán and view the United States as a place to advance their goals in Mexico. This involves earning money and gaining skills in Dallas that can be used in Mexico.

In sum, Lupe's agenda includes the following goals:

- to spend time with her sisters in the United States and then return to Mexico to be with her parents and other siblings
- to earn money in the United States so that she can return to Mexico and expand her business
- to educate her daughter so that she masters English and can be successful in Yucatán
- to maintain close contact to the other Yucatecos in Dallas

Juan's agenda includes the following:

- to learn English so that he can more easily converse with passengers in his taxicab in Cancún
- to earn money in the United States to improve his living situation in Cancún
- to educate his daughter so that she masters English and can be successful in Yucatán
- to expand his network and make friends who are not Yucatecan

Both partners thus have complementary migrant agendas in that they want to take advantage of opportunities in the United States in order to improve their chances for a bright future in Mexico. Their goals diverge in how they prioritize family, community, and maximization of prestige. For example, Lupe is more interested than Juan in maintaining family connections and close relationships with the people from Kaal. Juan wants to experience adventure and learn about the United States, perhaps to enhance his prestige in the context of the Kaal community. Juan wants to meet new people and broaden his social networks beyond the Yucatecan community. At the same time, Juan and Lupe negotiate these differences so that their plans remain compatible.

A Legal Pair: Lena and Mateo

Lena (53 years old) was born in Kaal exactly four days before Mateo, who was also born there. Lena is the oldest of five sisters. Her father, now deceased, was a *campesino* who farmed *milpa* and participated in a henequen-producing *ejido*. Her mother was a housewife, supplementing her husband's economic activity by assisting with *milpa* activities. Probably because Lena was the oldest and her siblings followed so soon after she was born, she was forced to work at the early age of ten. Although she can read and write today, she only attended eight days of school in her entire lifetime. Her first job was as a domestic in Kaal and she was paid only twelve pesos a month. Two years later, at the age of twelve, she worked in Mérida as a live-in domestic worker. She earned sixty pesos a month and was only allowed to leave the house one weekend a month on Saturday afternoon and was expected to be back in time for work on Monday morning. After holding several other domestic positions in Mérida, she returned to Kaal to work, and she kept working until she got married.

Mateo is also a first-born child; he is the oldest of seven siblings. His father was a *campesino* farming *milpa* and participating in an ejidal group. His mother was a housewife and helped her husband with his fieldwork. Now his father is retired and receives a government pension. Since he also gets funds from his four sons, Mateo's father no longer has to work.

Mateo completed elementary school through the fifth grade. When he was in sixth grade his mother became ill and his father needed economic assistance. As a result, he left school and began to work selling and delivering goods. In the morning hours he worked in the fields with his father. When he was eighteen he traveled to Belize for about six months and worked as an agricultural laborer. Just after he was married, he worked in Mérida for three years selling food from a hot dog cart. His next job was as a construction worker in Cancún. For four years he commuted back and forth every weekend so that he could spend weekends with his family in Kaal.

Mateo met Lena when he was making a delivery to her home. He later saw her at a dance in the plaza and asked her to dance, officially beginning their courtship. They married in 1967 and had their first child, Sara, in 1968. They had two more children in Mexico, a son born in 1968 and a daughter in 1972. In 1990 they had another son in Dallas.

Mateo's first attempt to go to the United States was in 1976. At first Alfredo, the pioneer migrant from Kaal, convinced Mateo to go to Dallas with him. Mateo returned home to tell Lena and, according to Mateo, she would not let him go. Later that year he convinced his wife to allow him to migrate and he made the journey northward with his brother and a friend from a nearby town. They were caught by the INS in southern Texas and sent back to Mexico. They tried again later and were deported once again by the INS. The third attempt, despite their getting robbed in Saltillo, was a success and Mateo made it to Dallas in 1977. He stayed there for three years and visited Kaal for two months in 1980. He tried to convince his wife to return to Dallas with him but she refused because she did not want to leave her children behind. Mateo continued to try to persuade his wife to go to Dallas and in 1984 she finally conceded and joined Mateo in the United States, leaving their three children with her parents in Kaal. She was able to secure a tourist visa so she did not have to cross the U.S.-Mexican border illegally.

Lena and Mateo lived and worked in Dallas for three years without their children. Lena was employed as a domestic and Mateo worked in various restaurants. Lena's and Mateo's children began to pressure them to return to Yucatán and they did so in 1987, fully intending to find jobs and remain with their children in Mexico. They stayed long enough to figure out that they were not able to earn even close to what they were accustomed to making in Dallas. They gave their daughter a *quinceañeara* and returned to Dallas with their teenage son shortly thereafter. Later, their youngest daughter joined them in Dallas. Sara, the eldest daughter, never wanted to come to the United States. She is now a nurse, living in Mérida with her husband and two daughters. To Lena's own surprise, because of her age and the fact that she had had a tubal ligation years earlier, she became pregnant and gave birth to a son in 1990.

When Mateo and Lena first arrived in Dallas they lived in a series of apartments close to or in the apartment complex where so many of the Yucatecan migrants live today. Now they live in their own house in a Dallas suburb. Lena works as a maid for a family in Dallas; she has had the same job since 1984. Mateo works as a groundskeeper at a golf course; he is one of the only Yucatecan men who does not work in a restaurant. Their oldest son works in a restaurant and their daughter works as a domestic. Although they live about twenty minutes away from the other Yucatecans, they maintain close contact; they visit the apartment complex almost daily. Lena's son's wife leaves her child with a woman from Kaal and she and her husband go to the apartment complex every day to pick him up and take him back home.

Mateo and Lena were both able to legalize under IRCA and Lena became a U.S. citizen in 1997. They petitioned for all of their children except Sara, who did not want U.S. residency, and their youngest son, who is already a U.S. citizen because he was born in the United States. Mateo has applied for citizenship but is waiting for his case to be processed. All family members in Dallas are now legal except for Lena's daughter-in-law (their son's wife), and their daughter's live-in boyfriend, both of whom have a possibility to legalize through their spouses.

In terms of migrant agendas, when I asked Mateo why he had come to the United States he simply said, "*para trabajar*" (to work). He later explained that he had earned only forty pesos a week in Mexico, not enough to buy books for the children's classes and food for the family. When the opportunity to migrate to the United States presented itself, he took it, planning to return to Kaal as soon as his children completed their studies. Later he realized that his children wanted to prepare for careers and that he would have to stay even longer in the United States if the family was to prosper. When his plan changed, he pressured his wife to join him so that he would not be alone in Dallas:

> I was all alone and if you are alone with your friends, you drink and spend. And then you realize you have no money. Before I drank quite a bit. The first thing I did was cash my paycheck and go directly to the post office to send money home. What was left I used to pay my rent and my food. I sent my money. But many don't do it that way. I lived with 'Luis.' 'Luis' as soon as he got his paycheck he started to drink and gamble, losing everything and afterwards saying 'daughter, I didn't send money.' It's that here if you don't watch your money, you will never get ahead even if you are earning a lot.

Having his wife with him in Dallas would not only prevent loneliness but also ensure that he did not waste money on beer and other diversions. Once Mateo saw that staying in Dallas was a long-term prospect, he sent for his wife.

Lena explained why she came to the United States:

> First to see it. And later because my husband wanted me to come because he was here for six years. And well...he didn't want to be alone, he wanted me to come. He was always sending for me but I did not want to go because my kids were little and I said 'I am not going because the kids are little and I am not going to leave them.' And he sent for me like three times with a man from Yaxcaba and I never wanted to come. But after I said 'OK, I am going to go.' And I came. But for the first month here I said 'I am not going to stay; I am just going to visit and then I will go back. I am going to be here for a few months and then I'll return.' But afterwards I met a Chicana, the manager there at the apartment complex, and we began to talk every day in the afternoon when she came to my house or I went to hers. We lived right across from her. And she told me that there was a lady looking for [a] work[er]. 'I worked with her,' she told me 'and she is looking for help. Do you want to go? Tell me and I'll call her.' And she called and the lady gave me two days of work. I think I was here a month. The lady gave me work and I stayed.

Lena has worked for this same woman for sixteen years. At first she cleaned house a few days and then later, when the woman gave birth to her son, Lena became the baby-sitter. Today all of the woman's children are grown but Lena still works for her full time as a housekeeper. Lena's case, like so many others, shows how migrant agendas are dynamic and flexible. Lena had originally planned to stay for a short time and then changed her mind. Part of her migrant agenda changed about one month after arriving in Dallas because, according to Lena, she found steady employment.

When I asked Lena and Mateo about their plans for the following year, they both said they were going to Kaal for two weeks during Christmas with their youngest son, Leo. As for the longer term, each mentioned Leo as an important factor in plans for the next five to ten years. Leo was born in the United States and is not used to living in Mexico. Lena said that she wants to stay in Dallas until Leo is eighteen, when he can get by without them. She explained to me that at eighteen he will be able decide if he is wants to return to Yucatán with her or if he wants to stay in Dallas. I asked if she would prefer to go back to Mexico sooner:

Lena: Yes, there are times, yes. Because there are times now that I get really tired working. Like they say, I'm getting old. I say that in ten years when I am almost sixty-five years old, well, who is going to give me work?

Rachel: But do you want Leo to change to a school in Mexico?

Lena: No.

Rachel: And your husband has the same plans? He wants the same thing or no?

Lena: Yes, this is what we want. This is what we are planning; when Leo is older we are going there for a while. And then return here . . . like that, no?

Rachel: Both?

Lena: Both.

Rachel: Both, to live in both places?

Lena: What we are thinking is to save a little money so that we can live well there and afterwards return here again just to visit because like I said, at that age we are not going to be able to do anything. (laughs)

To Lena, residing but not working in the United States means she is visiting. Once she and her husband are retired, according to Lena, they plan on going back and forth. Mateo told me something similar. He, too, wants to stay in the United States until Leo finishes school, and then to spend time in both Dallas and Kaal. I asked Mateo if he would prefer to be in Yucatán or Dallas in ten years. At first, he said that if possible, he would prefer to be in Mexico, even though his three children in the United States will probably want to stay here. Later in the interview he said,

To me it is the same to live here or there. Because I am used to both places. If I go there I am used to it.

> If I come here I am used to it. Or I could be there for a time…

The desire to go back and forth, rather than remaining in Dallas, implies a transnational ideology. It also reflects hard economic realities: earnings are too low in Mexico to stay there permanently. Lena and Mateo's family also spans two nations. Their oldest daughter is a Mexican national with no desire to migrate to the United States. Their youngest son is a U.S. citizen with little experience living in Mexico. Thus although migration may begin for economic reasons, the presence of family members on both sides of the border is a factor keeping migrants connected to Dallas as well as to Kaal. In Lena and Mateo's case, there are property considerations as well. They own houses in both Kaal and Dallas, making it convenient to live their lives in both places.

In Dallas, Lena and Mateo maintain close contact with others from Kaal. They visit the apartment complex regularly and keep up with all of the news and gossip. Both call their parents and daughter in Yucatán on a regular basis. They have managed to secure tourist visas for their elderly mothers, who have visited Dallas several times. The couple also tries to visit Kaal whenever possible and they like to take their son Leo along so that he can gain exposure to life in Yucatán.

Lena became a U.S. citizen in April 1998; Mateo is a legal resident and has applied for U.S. citizenship. When I interviewed them, they were both frustrated because of recent legislation that had adversely affected their youngest daughter. Their oldest son arrived in Dallas in time to legalize under the IRCA amnesty. The younger daughter arrived in the United States afterwards and without documents, and Lena and Mateo had filed for her legal residency. Legislation that went into effect in January 1998 forced undocumented people with pending residency applications to leave the United States while their cases were being processed. Their daughter left Dallas in September 1997 and was still in Kaal in May 1998 when I conducted the interviews. They were beginning to worry that she would never be able to legalize because it had been so long. With this looming large in her thoughts,

Lena worried about how difficult it would be for most of the Yucatecans to legalize:

> Well, it hurts me. Because who doesn't want to have the right to be here, you know? Everyone wants to have their rights so that they won't have problems with anyone. Sometimes I get mad when I hear the INS changed it like this, the INS did this or that and I ask 'why all of the animosity? Why so much animosity if we are all human beings?' But those are the laws; first, those are the laws of this nation, of this land and second, well, I think we have to do it that way. We can't change anything. We can't do anything about it.

Eventually, the daughter did obtain legal residency, and she arrived in Dallas in July of 1998, so this particular story has a happy ending. All the family members in Dallas are now there legally, and having rights in the United States gives them a sense of empowerment. The day before I interviewed Lena there was a bond election in Dallas. Mateo berated her for not voting, even though she was a newly naturalized U.S. citizen. Lena said that she did not vote because she did not know the procedure, but she expressed interest in voting in the future.

To sum up, both Lena and Mateo share basic aspects of their migrant agenda; they want:

- their youngest son, Leo, to complete his education in the United States
- to work hard and earn and save money for their youngest son and for their retirement
- to visit and maintain contact with people from Kaal in both Dallas and Yucatán
- to legalize the entire family
- to spend their retirement shuttling back and forth between Dallas and Kaal

This couple gives priority to maintaining extended family ties. They also wish to sustain their connections to Kaal and the community of Kaal in Dallas. Their last priority, but also important, is maximization of prestige within the context of the Kaal community—on both sides of the border.

A Legal–Undocumented Pair: Melba and Felipe

Melba and Felipe are both 37 years old; they were born and raised in Kaal. Melba comes from a large family; she is one of ten siblings. Her father, now retired as a result of a stroke in 1997, was a *campesino* who farmed both *milpa* and henequen when Melba was growing up. More recently, he bought a truck and started cutting, transporting, and selling wood throughout the area.

When Melba was a child she had many responsibilities. She was in charge of two of her younger sisters, and bathed and watched them during the day. She also had to wash all of the clothing for the entire family. Probably for this reason, she only completed school through the fourth grade. When she was fifteen she found employment as a domestic in Kaal for a family that lived near the plaza. After about a year and a half at this job, she went to Mérida where she worked as a live-in maid. She could only visit her family in Kaal every two weeks and, as a result, only lasted six months in that job. She returned to Kaal and worked in several different homes as a domestic until she married her husband and became a housewife. When her husband left for the United States the first time she did not go with him; it was not until 1991 that she joined him in Dallas. In Dallas she has worked as a domestic, and when I met her she was a baby-sitter for several Yucatecan children there.

Felipe is the first-born and only son in a family of four children. His father was the commissioner of an ejidal group and farmed both henequen and *milpa*. His mother helped her husband and made *rebozos* for sale. Felipe attended *primaria* and *secundaria* all the while helping his father in the fields each morning before school. After completing *secundaria* he worked for the government in a literacy program in which he was required to travel to other towns and teach people how to read. When he was twenty he began selling sodas in Kaal and then quit to become a cook in a restaurant in Mérida. He kept this job for five years and traveled daily between Kaal and Mérida. His next job was in Cancún, where for about a year and a half he worked in construction. Felipe's first trip to the U.S. was in 1988. His destination was not Dallas but California, the other major receiving area for people from Kaal. He stayed in California for three years and worked as an agricultural laborer. During those three years he made one three-week visit to Kaal in 1990 for the May fiesta. In 1991 he migrated from California to Dallas and has remained there ever since.

Felipe and Melba met in Kaal. Melba was a good friend of two of Felipe's younger sisters and visited them often. Felipe liked her and they began their courtship. They married two years later in 1984. They had their first child in Mexico in 1985; their twin daughters were born in Dallas in 1992. Felipe was able to legalize his own status under IRCA legislation; he has petitioned for his wife and son's legal residency and they are waiting for that to be processed. Their twin daughters are U.S. citizens because they were born in Dallas.

Felipe said that he came to the United States "to try and better my life." Neither his wife nor his family wanted him to go but he had the urge to make the trip. Whenever friends and acquaintances returned from the United States to visit Mexico, they would tell him how wonderful the United States was and encourage him to go. Also, he said the difficult economic situation in Kaal was a motivating factor.

When he got to California, Felipe had problems because he drank a lot and found it hard to save money to send home to his family in Kaal. This is why he decided to send for his wife to join him:

> Well, I was in California alone for a year and a half and I felt bad because I left them there and the truth is that there were times in California where I... I drank a lot. And I hadn't sent money and when I arrived in Mexico to visit for the first time, she and my son were alone; it would be better if I brought them to Texas. I sent for the two of them and they

came here and it is better to have them with me.
This way I can see my son grow up and I can keep
an eye on him and everything. Now, I am here seeing that he is doing his schoolwork and everything.
It is better to be together than separated. It's hard.

When Melba joined her husband in Dallas she was the
first person in her family to migrate to the United States.
When I asked if she came because she wanted to or just because her husband sent for her, she replied:

Well, yes, I wanted to come because he sent me almost no money. And I said 'now an opportunity has
come that he sent to get me' and I said 'I'm going.' I
said that if I stay there he is not going to send me
any money so it's better that I go. And that's why I
came. I came with my son. Because my parents and
my oldest sister didn't want me to bring him (Arturo). They were afraid at that time and they said
that I am going to cross over the river and drown
and who knows what, and it isn't true—I passed
over, but in tire tubes. It was a river with lots of stuff
at the bottom, and so we passed over sitting on
makeshift seats on the tire tubes. The river wasn't
deep. When I got there I realized that you could
cross that river walking. And I brought Arturo. I
came with him and it was better.

Soon after arriving in Dallas, Melba became pregnant, and
she gave birth to twins in May 1992. She needed help with
the two babies so she sent for an unmarried younger sister,
Nidia, to come and assist her. Nidia came to Dallas and
moved in with Melba and Felipe. Eventually, Nidia met and
then married another Yucatecan; when she had a child she
sent for another unmarried sister, Carla, to come help her
with child care responsibilities. At present, two of Melba's
sisters and two of her brothers live in Dallas. Carla and her
younger brother live with Melba and Felipe.

Both Felipe and Melba had similar short-term plans. At
the time of the interview, Melba had been in the United
States for seven years and was eager to visit her family in

Kaal. In those seven years Felipe had made almost yearly visits to the town. Melba did not want to visit because to return without papers might endanger her chances of legalizing. So, rather than take a risk, she decided to wait it out in Dallas and live with the sadness of missing her parents and siblings. The first thing that Melba said when I asked about plans for the following year was that if her papers came she was going to go visit Kaal in May. She was hopeful that she would receive her visa by then. Felipe told me that he had definite plans to go to Kaal for the fiesta in May and intended to take the twins with him. He also hoped that Melba's papers would come through, and felt bad that she had not been able to visit Kaal. Both agreed that if the papers were not ready that she would stay in Dallas, for neither wanted to take a risk that she might endanger her chances for legal residency.

When asked about plans for the longer term, both agreed that they wanted to buy a house in Kaal so that they will have a place to go when they are there. They disagreed about plans in Dallas. Felipe is tired of renting and wants to look into buying a house, but Melba thinks that a house will bring too many expenses and instead wants to stay where they are. This was the only disagreement. Both Felipe and Melba had plans to live a binational life. As Felipe said:

> I would like to be here for a time and then go to Yucatán to live for a while too. Then after a year or a year and a half in Mexico come back here again. Or go back to Mexico and stay for six months and come back here for a little bit and go back again.

Melba expressed similar sentiments, although she imagines shorter visits to Mexico. When I asked if there was a chance that she would stay in Mexico, we had this exchange:

Melba: Well, perhaps I would stay for May vacation. I don't know. If I had a job I would only stay for a month. If I had five days of domestic work I would stay only a month. I would not stay for the whole vacation.

Rachel: Yes. But you would not quit your job and stay in Yucatán?

Melba: No, because if I have the opportunity to work as a domestic [here], knowing that I will earn well [in Dallas] I would go to Yucatán every year. If I had papers I would go every year.

Melba and Felipe want to stay in the United States partly because they can earn a better living here. Both think about shuttling back and forth; the only difference is that Felipe talks about spending longer periods in Mexico. Another factor likely to influence their decision is their children. Felipe said that even though his son Arturo spent the first five years of his life in Mexico, he is more accustomed to life in Dallas. He did not think that Arturo would be able to get used to Mexico. When I interviewed Arturo, he expressed a similar sentiment:

Arturo: There's more chances here than in Mexico. I feel better here even though my grandparents are there. I just feel right here.

Rachel: How old were you when you came here? You were a little kid.

Arturo: I think I was five. I was getting out of kinder[garten]

Rachel: Do you remember anything about Kaal?

Arturo: Umm...like sometimes my mom tells me, "do you remember this lady?" and I say "I don't know her" and she says "how can you forget?"

Rachel: But you were little.

Arturo: That's what I tell her. I forgot about some of my aunts, I forgot their names. Sometimes they got to remind me.

Rachel: You have a lot of aunts and uncles because your mom has ten brothers and sisters! Do you want to visit?

Arturo: Um hmm.

Rachel: But would it be a place that you would actually live?

Arturo: For a little while, yeah, but I feel better here.

Rachel: You feel better here...you are an American kid?

Arturo: No!

Rachel: Do you feel like an American kid or no?

Arturo: No. I'm still Mexican but I just like it here.

This conversation was in English, but Arturo is completely bilingual. He speaks only Spanish with his parents because they do not know English. He speaks both English and Spanish with his school friends. It is likely that Arturo's much-younger twin sisters, who were born in the United States, will be even more oriented to life in this country and less comfortable in Mexico. At this point, however, they speak only Spanish.

Felipe and Melba maintain constant contact with people from Kaal. Felipe visits once a year and Melba calls home every two weeks. They live in the central apartment complex and all of their closest friends are from Yucatán. Felipe told me that he felt he was a part of the Kaal community in Yucatán. He pointed out, however, that being a migrant changes how non-migrants in Kaal view him—and he, too, feels different from the stay-at-homes:

> You feel, you feel a little rejected when you arrive. But yes, not rejected . . . like they don't trust you . . . like they see you and they don't know you. They look at you differently. But they accept you afterwards. Yes, they accept you the same way. When you were born there they accept you. And the most important thing is to be humble when you arrive; if just because you are in the United States you arrive showing off and saying 'I have money,' they are going to hate you. No one is going to like you. But if you arrive and you are nice to everyone and you greet everyone, they will treat you the same. There are many people that live here and arrive there and try to show off to the people there. It is not good. The people reject them. No one will accept them.

Felipe also has developed ties in Dallas, and explained how in his job as a cook he serves the Dallas community and contributes to the city's economic well-being. Melba, however, felt less identification with the broader Dallas community:

> Because I wasn't born here, well, I don't feel part of the Dallas community. With the Yucatecos I think [I feel part of the community], only with the Yucatecos that live here and that's it. Well, only here [in the apartment complex]; that's it. Not all of Dallas. I speak with Lidia and Doña Maria; I speak with the Yucatecas and that's all, but not with all of them. I don't think I feel part of it; the truth is I don't know.

Felipe is a legal resident and he had applied for citizenship in order to legalize his son and his wife. At the time of the interview, the family was waiting for Melba and Arturo's legalization papers to be processed so that they could finally visit Yucatán. Note the motivation behind legalization. At least for Felipe and Melba, it had nothing to do with the desire to assimilate into U.S. society or to cut ties to Mexico. Quite the contrary. For Felipe and Melba, legalization would allow the maintenance of closer contact with Mexico. Felipe and Melba also want to ensure that they and their son Arturo have certain rights, such as access to health care, education, and legal employment, which are not granted to undocumented residents in the United States. The couple are clear about wanting to maintain dual nationality. According to Felipe:

> Sometimes when you are a citizen from here and not in Mexico they give you problems there. On the other hand, having dual nationality, you can stay in Mexico too. They don't say anything to you. I feel like this (with dual nationality)—it is like you are Mexican. You have not denounced your nationality. You still feel Mexican. But it is kind of hard if you are a citizen here and not there because you can't have property there; you can't have anything there. Nothing. On the other hand, with Mexican citizenship you can have your own house there, a small business, whatever you want to do you can do. That's why I say it's good to have citizenship in both.

Melba said that although she wants to be a legal permanent resident, she does not want to become a U.S. citizen. If it becomes necessary for her to apply for citizenship, she also wants to maintain her rights in Mexico:

> I have to return to my country where I was born. I am not going to lose my traditions. I was born there and I have to go to visit my town. I can't forget. Of course not.

In sum, Melba and Felipe's migrant agendas converge. They both intend:

- to legalize Melba and Arturo's status in the United States
- that Melba will visit Kaal as soon as she has legal residency
- to visit and maintain contact with people from Kaal in Dallas and in Yucatán
- to purchase a home in Kaal
- to earn enough money in Dallas so they can spend time in both Dallas and Kaal

The only notable differences are that Melba resists Felipe's plan to buy a house in Dallas, and Melba's intended visits to Yucatán would be shorter than Felipe's. In maintaining ties to both Kaal and Dallas, Melba prioritizes family connections while Felipe emphasizes community ties.

Migrant–Non Migrant Pair: Jorge and Blanca

Jorge is the youngest brother of José, the transnational man whose life story was told in Chapter 5. Jorge's father was a peasant farmer; his mother took care of household responsibilities, including raising seven children. Jorge finished *secundaria* and then worked as a blacksmith's apprentice for two and a half years in Mérida, traveling between Kaal and Mérida every day. When he lost his job—the business was seriously damaged by Hurricane Gilbert—Jorge asked his brother (who was in the U.S.) for help in migrating to Dallas. His brother obliged, sending money to pay for the trip, and Jorge arrived in Dallas for the first time in 1990. He lived with his brother and worked as a dishwasher in a popular Dallas restaurant. Two years later, in 1992, he went back to Kaal for the first time, spending two weeks with his wife and family. Six months later he decided to visit again, that time for a month. After the second trip, one of his brothers died in Kaal and Jorge returned there to attend the funeral. The entire time that Jorge has been in Dallas he has lived with his brothers, nephews, or male friends from Kaal.

Blanca is one of eight children. Her parents separated when she was twelve, and she was raised by her father. She attended elementary school only until the third grade because she had to work to help support her family. Her father drank a lot and she had a very difficult and unhappy childhood. Her first job was as a live-in domestic in Mérida. She had several other domestic positions and worked until she moved in with Jorge.

Jorge and Blanca met through his sister. They courted and six months later, when she became pregnant with their first child, she moved in with him into his parents' house. Although Blanca wanted to get married, Jorge did not. To this day they are not married. As a result, Blanca's father refuses to talk to her and they have not spoken in years. She had another child several years later. Blanca lived with her in-laws in their house until May 1999 when Jorge went back to Kaal to live.

Jorge said that he initially came to the United States "to have a better life in the future." In 1998, when I interviewed him, his plan was to return to Mexico to look for a job and settle with his common-law wife and children. He claimed that he was returning permanently and that if he came back to the United States it would be to visit and not to work.

In Dallas, Jorge worked and socialized with other Yucatecos. His brothers, nephew, and niece were in Dallas and so he not only had friends but family in Dallas. He called his wife often and sent money and gifts to Kaal on a regular basis.

In 1998, when I asked Jorge if he planned to have his wife and children join him in Dallas he gave an emphatic "no":

> Because I am here illegally, right? And if tomorrow comes and I lose my job what am I going to do if I

> have my family here? I am going to be without a job,
> do you understand? I have my brothers here and
> they help me. But it isn't the same as being responsi-
> ble for an entire family. And if I have no job and I
> have no papers and she has no papers, what would
> we do? I am alone here; between three or four friends
> the rent is less. With my family here I would have to
> pay all of the rent, do you understand? And this is a
> problem that I don't want. If tomorrow I lose my job,
> I have a little money in my pocket to go to Mexico.
> But with my family, no. I would need a lot of money
> to pay their tickets and everything.

Jorge did not have documentation and had no real possibility
of legalizing himself or his family, and this was the principal
reason he did not want his family to join him in Dallas. Jorge
did go back to Kaal in 1999, with the intention of staying for
good. Jorge, Blanca, and their two children moved into the
house he had built next to his parents' and Jorge found a job
in a large tourist hotel in Mérida. But his return was short-
lived. Jorge went back to Dallas in January 2000 despite his
plans to the contrary.

Blanca never went to Dallas, and as a non-migrant did
not, obviously, have a migrant agenda. But stay-at-home
wives have life projects that can strongly influence their
spouse's migrant agenda and migration patterns. Blanca did
not want her husband to go to Dallas at first, but he convinced her that he could earn money there. She wanted to
go with him but he refused:

> *Blanca:* Well, I wanted to go afterwards but I couldn't.
> Well, not because of our son but rather because he said
> no, it is very risky to go there ... I was dying to go, but
> no. It's that he does not support me. Because my sister-
> in-law, she went. She left behind her one-and-a-half-
> year-old daughter. She was in the United States for six
> years until she came back here.
>
> *Rachel:* And when she went, you wanted to go too?
>
> *Blanca:* Yes, but he never supported my going. Yes, many
> women go. Just a little while ago a few women went.
> Well, I wanted to go. Not so long ago I asked him "why

don't you want me to go?" He said, "no, it's that I'll be there only a little bit more and I will come back (to Kaal)." But he does not stay. A little bit of time and he leaves again. Well, I think he has gotten used to the form of life there. Life here is very different. I think that life is very hard here. There they have to cook their own food and wash their own clothing but it is very comfortable there. They don't have to wash clothes by hand like they do here or mop the floor like we do here. Right? I think that he has become accustomed to the comforts there.

This is a case of agendas that are clearly in conflict. Blanca wants Jorge to stay in Kaal and work. She has offered to get a job to supplement his wages. Jorge does not want to stay in Kaal (although at one point he did) and he does not want Blanca to have a job in Mexico, or to migrate to Dallas. Both want the family to prosper but both have different ideas about how to do this. Since Blanca is not legally married to Jorge she is in a particularly vulnerable position. Jorge continues to resist the idea of marriage.

Jorge's migrant agenda includes the following:

- to stay in Mexico only as long as he decides he wants to at the time
- to migrate to Dallas alone without the burden of spouse and children
- to maintain contact with his family in Kaal
- to maintain relationships with Yucatecos in Dallas
- to earn money so that his family can prosper

Blanca's goals relative to Jorge's migrant agenda are:

- to join Jorge in Dallas with or without her children
- to earn money so the family can prosper

Unlike the three preceding cases, Blanca is not a migrant and the couple has not worked out a migrant agenda that is compatible with the life projects of both parties. Jorge does not want his wife with him in Dallas and he has made this clear to her in his refusal to sponsor her migration. He is responsible and maintains his family financially, but he prefers the freedom of being in Dallas without his wife and children there. This explains why he changed his mind about remaining in Kaal with his family. He feels that as long as he is remitting money to his family he is fulfilling his obligations—and that it is up to him to decide whether to be in Kaal or Dallas.

DISCUSSION OF THE CASES

The case studies make clear that migrant spouses must cooperate to at least some degree in order to pursue goals that are for the good of the family, however these are defined. If men drink too much, this directly challenges the stated agendas for their family, which in every case involved improving the lives of all its members. Both men and women criticize excessive drinking by males even when those doing the criticizing are themselves drinkers. Mateo and Felipe, for example, both talked about how they wanted their wives to join them in Dallas so that they would not drink. Their wives agreed that drinking was a threat to the family welfare, and saw their arrival in Dallas as a way to keep their husbands from drinking too much and squandering family funds.

That three of the couples generally had complementary migrant agendas may result from the fact that they agreed to be together in Dallas in the first place. Most Yucatecan men in Dallas do not have their wives with them. Men with migrant wives probably already have a propensity towards marital cooperation that their married counterparts with spouses in Mexico may lack.

The case studies also suggest that wherever husbands or wives plan to live in the future, they see themselves as important and active members of their family units. Geographic separation may be unpleasant but it is usually viewed as an acceptable and realistic option.

Each of the couples residing in Dallas wanted to legalize their status in the United States. Their goals of legalizing were mainly based on a desire to maintain stronger ties to Yucatán. As Jacqueline Hagan found (1994) among Guatemalans in

Houston, for Yucatecans in Dallas, legalization is a means to achieve transnational migrant agendas. My sense is that, once they obtain a "green card," women are more likely than men to intend to live in Kaal and visit the United States. This is a topic that clearly requires more study.

Conclusion: Yucatecan Men and Women in Dallas

The study of migration and gender, it is important to remember, is not just a matter of adding females to a study sample, but of viewing gender, both male and female, as an important principle of social organization. Thus, in this chapter I have explored how migration is experienced by men and women because of their gender. I have also illustrated how married pairs negotiate and renegotiate their migrant agendas. These negotiations continue over time—they are, in truth, a lifelong process.

In the workforce, the division of labor by gender in American society has important implications for the kinds of jobs that Yucatecan men and women have in Dallas. So do Yucatecan cultural ideas about *casa* and *calle*, and the segregation of the sexes. Thus, the women do not search for restaurant employment despite the demand for employees. And although the men learn how to cook, clear tables, and wash dishes in their places of employment they do not use these skills at home if there is a woman in the household. The result is that working Yucatecan women must endure a double day. It appears that one reason women do not envision long-term settlement in the United States is that a return to Mexico would significantly reduce their workload. Also, they face difficulties securing domestic employment in Dallas. Although domestic employment may be socially isolating for women, the social isolation that accompanies unemployment is far worse (cf. Brettell 1982:30).

Yucatecans view migration not as just a geographical event but also as a means of social mobility (Ho 1999:50) and both men and women agree that, in cases where migrant couples choose to live separately, men should be the ones to stay and work in the United States. Men are considered to be the primary breadwinners in Yucatán, and often the reason they migrate in the first place is to provide for their families. Many married migrants with wives in Mexico live in uncomfortable, crowded conditions so that they can send more money to their spouses in Kaal. Women, even those who work in Dallas, continue to view men as the primary breadwinners. Thus, at least in principle, the main responsibility for earning a wage falls on male shoulders. And because women are not viewed as responsible for supporting their families, they are granted the right to at least entertain the thought of permanent return.

The reality is that many Yucatecan women in Dallas work and their income is necessary for household survival. Thus although women think about permanent return to Mexico, only time will tell if they really do so. One mitigating factor is their English proficient children, who often have far more experience and success operating within U.S. institutions than their parents. Many second-generation children, especially those enrolled in school, do not want to live in Yucatán, although they are interested in maintaining ties there. As these children mature, it will be important to see how their agendas affect those of their parents.

Perhaps at this early stage of migration, when women represent only a small portion of the migrant population, it is not surprising that married migrants have similar agendas. The process of wives joining husbands requires intense spousal cooperation. Even when the decision for a wife to join her husband is made by only one of them, it takes the cooperation of both to actually make it happen. Moreover, single women need familial cooperation and support both in Dallas and Kaal. Young women wishing to migrate without parents are unlikely to do so unless they have relatives in Dallas who can supervise them and reassure their non-migrating parents that their "honor will be upheld." Their migration and their ability to remain in Dallas depend on their willingness to cooperate in the household of sponsoring relatives.

Undoubtedly, at a later stage of the migration to Dallas—as networks intensify, migration becomes an increasingly generalized process, and women are a higher proportion of the migrant population—there will be changes. It is likely that more women, in the future, will arrive on their own. Also, as the migration progresses, women's employment networks will expand, leading to higher rates of female employment. This could have the effect of creating more household conflict as women begin to assert themselves by refusing to work a double day.

7

Conclusion

This study has shown how of a group of people from Kaal, Yucatán, live their lives across borders, and do so despite the costs and risks. As such, it is a contribution to a growing body of literature that takes seriously the role of migrants and other workers as important transnational actors. It also offers a perspective that views migrants' agendas as not only shaped by structural forces but also as having the potential to transform the social arenas in which they operate.

YUCATECAN MIGRANTS AND SOCIAL CHANGE

In one sense, it can be said that by leaving Kaal and going to Dallas, migrants are not only operating in a system of global capitalism that has set the stage for their migration, but they also help reproduce the social systems of global capitalism and the nation-state. Migration from northern Yucatán to Dallas has its roots in the employment structure of Kaal, which, as a community in Mexico, occupies a position as labor supplier and producer of raw materials in the international division of labor. The migrants go to Dallas, a city in a core nation-state where wages and profits are high and the economic infrastructure is strong and that has a thriving labor market with a high demand for service workers. Deeply-rooted and persistent structural inequality, in other words, underpins the migration. Moreover, it could be argued that by participating in labor migration, migrants are reinforcing the very conditions that cause it in the first place. Yet a closer look at the lives of the migrants reveals that they are not simply passive players who respond to structural forces and inequalities. They are active agents who, whether consciously or not, have challenged the status quo. By examining border crossing and transnational migration we can see how migrants have the potential to transform society by developing new social norms and social practices that facilitate pursuit of their life projects.

Border Crossing

The words of "Los mandados," a popular Mexican song, illustrate the sentiments of many migrants who cross the border without documents. Although being detained and deported by the border patrol is a frightening and humiliating experience, a sense of pride and persistence leads migrants to pursue their migrant agendas in the face of adversity:

Los Mandeados (The Commanded)

Without even thinking twice about it, I swam across the Rio Grande.

The INS threw me out in Nogales, I crossed again and then they threw me out in Juarez.

From there I went to Tamaulipas and disguised myself as a gringo by coloring my hair, since I don't speak any English I got thrown out again.

I have smuggled myself as a wetback across Mexicali and San Luis Rio Colorado and I never gave up getting to the other side.

I know every part of the border, every path, river and canal from Tijuana to Reynosa, from Matamoros to Juarez, from Piedras Negras to El Paso and from Agua Prieta to Nogales.

The INS threw me out three hundred times; but I was never tamed, they were under my command.

Their fellow countrymen will pay for the beatings that they gave me.

Surreptitious border crossings are an unfortunate fact of life for most Yucatecan migrants. Political borders, I suggest, are the ultimate symbols of the modern system of a globe divided by nation-states. The Yucatecan migrants, in both a symbolic and a literal sense, challenge that system by crossing the U.S.-Mexican border without documents (see Adler 2000; Kearney 1991; Rodríguez 1996). The repeated act of crossing the border without papers, even though a violation of law(s), has led to new norms whereby the crossing is viewed by millions of Mexican nationals as legitimate and justified. Among Kaaleños the crossing act is treated as normal and routine, even though the danger and risks are always considered and the decision to cross is carefully thought about beforehand. Border crossing, in short, has become conventional because of the collective actions of migrants. Moreover, alternative, underground practices have developed to facilitate the border-crossing process. The sale of false documents, fraudulent marriage arrangements, border smuggling operations, guest houses on the Mexican side of the border, safe houses on the United States side—all of these practices flourish because of the alternative social system that migrants have created through active pursuit of their goals. Another song, "Long Live the Wetbacks," illustrates this process:

Vivan los Mojados (Long Live the Wetbacks)

Because we are the wetbacks the law is always looking for us.

Because we are illegal, and we don't speak English, the insolent gringos throw us out. But we come back.

When they throw a few of us out in Laredo, ten more enter through Mexicali.

If they throw out a few of us in Tijuana, six more enter through Nogales.

There is no telling how many of us enter every month.

Our problem is easy to solve, give us an American woman to marry so that we can get our green card and divorce her.

When the wetbacks finally go on strike, they will leave and not return.

Who will harvest the onions, lettuce, beets, lemons
   and the grapefruit?
Everything will spoil.
Long live all of the wetbacks who are going to immi-
   grate, those who are coming for vacation, those
   who are about to cross, and those who will marry
   to legalize their status.

Popular rhetoric in the United States has it that crossing
the border by undocumented migrants is dangerous for U.S.
legal residents, destructive to property, wildlife, and the
economy, and uncontrollable. Government leaders have
tried to find solutions to this problem; some have suggested
closing the border, while others support opening the border
and/or instituting a guest-worker program similar to the
Bracero program that was enacted during the Second World
War. Migrants have normalized an "illegal" act to such a degree that it has become part of the status quo for millions
and extremely difficult for nation-states to control.

Transnational Migration

Transnational migration can be viewed as representing opposition to the modern nation-state system because, according to the dominant ideology associated with that system,
individuals can only be loyal to one nation-state at a time.
Thus in the United States, migrants are expected to assimilate into the dominant society by learning English, adopting
the values of U.S. society, and internalizing and abiding by
the norms and laws of the nation-state. When legal residents
become U.S. citizens, they must officially renounce their affiliation to their nations of origin.

Transnationalism can be a means for migrants to protect
themselves from racism and discrimination they experience
in the United States. Migrants can insulate themselves from
xenophobia by maintaining ties to their hometowns and using their social networks to pursue their migrant agendas.

Despite social pressures to assimilate, many migrants in
the United States do so only on their own terms, all the
while maintaining social fields across borders. Yet another
recent song, "Countryman to Countryman," protests labor

exploitation in the United States and calls for a world without borders:

De Paisano a Paisano (Countryman to Countryman)

Like an eagle in flight . . . , defying borders, defending honor.

I have spent my life exploring other lands to give my children a better tomorrow.

If death finds me, wrap me in my flag and take me there [to Mexico] and sing my national anthem ten times, if they buried me here [in the U.S.] I would die twice.

Countryman to countryman, brother to brother, because we want to come here to work the border patrol wages a war against us.

But they can't tame us.

Countryman to countryman, brother to brother, it is the men who cry, how my country hurts when my people cry far from home.

Countryman to countryman, I ask your bosses who harvests the crops, who cleans the hotels and restaurants, and who kills themselves working in construction while the boss yells at them from his luxurious mansion?

Many times they don't even pay us, and to add salt to the wound, they call the INS.

If only my song could demolish the borders, so that all the world could live under one single flag, in one single nation.

The repeated, collective actions of migrants have led to new social conventions. As migrants send money to and call and visit their places of origin, business enterprises have emerged to accommodate this transnational activity. In Dallas, money transfer and bus companies have stepped in to provide the services necessary for migrants to maintain a transnational lifestyle. As I described in Chapter 5, there are places in Dallas that have become "Mexican spaces" because migrants and their children have appropriated them. Among them is the *pulga* (flea market) in Dallas, where

Anglos are a minority; English is barely heard; and Mexican music, art, religious symbols, and clothing styles are normative. To remain profitable, many businesses in Dallas have had to adapt to a Spanish-speaking clientele by hiring bilingual cashiers and purchasing stock (such as *tortillas* or religious candles) that appeal to their clientele. Dallas has changed owing to the actions of migrants who, to pursue their migrant agendas, have decided to maintain ties to their places of origin and continue their cultural traditions in the receiving area.

That migrants maintain ties to their homelands while they are residing in the United States also challenges notions of assimilation, which are part of the dominant ideology of the United States (see Basch, Glick-Schiller, and Blanc 1995: 40–45). Indeed, to combat this resistance to assimilation there has been public outcry, in some regions of the country, to cut off funding for programs that encourage the maintenance of migrants' cultural heritage. In California and Arizona, bilingual education has lost its public funding, and the justification has been that migrants must learn English in order to assimilate. According to critics of bilingual education, it prevents the rapid adoption of English and prevents migrants from becoming "Americanized." I would argue that the renewed push for migrants to assimilate is in part a backlash against the anti-assimilative effects of transnationalism. In other words, as many migrants continue to speak their native languages (and prefer that business and social service discourse be conducted in that language), vote in other countries, and send money to foreign lands, many native-born Americans view transnationalism as anti-American and see it as preventing assimilation.

Sending nation-states have also responded to migrant transnationalism by trying to take advantage of migrants' connections to their homelands. Mexico, Guatemala, El Salvador, Haiti, and the Dominican Republic (among others) have all recently passed legislation allowing migrants who become U.S. citizens to retain their home country nationality and/or citizenship. Migrant remittances are critical for these nation-states, and many governments have recognized the benefits of encouraging migrants to remain politically (and economically) involved in their native countries.

That so many countries have changed their policies to accommodate migrants again represents the impact of migrants' actions. Transnationalism by migrants has led to
social transformation.

FINAL THOUGHTS: WILL
TRANSNATIONALISM LAST?

Transnationalism is alive and well among contemporary
Yucatecan migrants in Dallas, but what about the future? Will
they, over time, continue to maintain social ties across borders, or will many return permanently or remain in the
United States and sever ties to Yucatán? Will this lead to the
demise of the transnational social field? And what about
the second generation? Will the children of migrants who are
born in the United States continue to participate in the transnational social field created by their parents? Nancy Foner's
(2000) historical, comparative approach to second-generation
transnationalism raises another question: what can the experiences of Italian and Jewish second generations a century
ago tell us about the fate of the Yucatecans in Dallas?

Second-generation Jews and Italians did not remain
transnational. For Jews, this was undoubtedly related to the
Holocaust and the virulent anti-Semitism that festered for
centuries in Eastern Europe. Indeed, as in the case of my
own Polish grandmother, many Jews left Europe well before
World War II because of the discrimination that they faced
in Eastern Europe. These immigrants had no desire to maintain ties to anyone besides family members left behind—
once the entire family had migrated, ties to Europe were cut.
But transnational ties among second-generation Italians,
whose parents had strong emotional connections to the
homeland, disintegrated as well (Foner 2000:239). Foner at-
tributes some of this to assimilation. As Italians and Jews attended American schools and became proficient in English,
they came to view themselves as Americans (Ibid:239–240).
But there is another factor that mediated against second-
generation transnationalism, and it is crucial to the comparison of Yucatecans with Jews and Italians. In the 1920s,
restrictive immigration laws prohibited "fresh recruits"

from replenishing the Italian and Jewish immigrant communities (Ibid:240). This situation is remarkably different from the case of Yucatecans in Dallas. Immigration laws are much more lax today than they were in the 1920s, facilitating continued migration to the United States. Furthermore, in the Yucatecan case, migrants are often undocumented. The relative ease of undocumented entry for Mexicans in general (because of the proximity of the border) ensures a steady flow of new immigrants. These new migrants are likely to keep transnationalism alive in the "transnational village" (Levitt 2001). The second generation is more likely to participate in transnationalism if it remains a viable option to do so.

The Yucatecan 1.5 generation (children who migrated when they were young) and second-generation youth are vulnerable to experiencing segmented assimilation in the United States, whereby they assimilate, not into the middle classes, but into the urban underclass (Portes and Zhou 1993; Portes 1995). The parents of the second generation are clearly in the bottom part of the hourglass economy and it is unlikely that they will experience much upward social mobility. The second generation attends blighted schools with few positive role models to facilitate their movement out of the low-end service sector.

Yet unlike their immigrant parents, who perceive their lives in Dallas as an improvement over the poverty of Kaal, the second generation has been socialized into the American consumption culture. It is likely that if they do not achieve financial success in the mainstream U.S. economy that they will use the transnational social field to their own advantage. Proficiency in Spanish and English and the ability to function in two distinct cultural settings place the second generation in a potential ethnic broker role that could be used to their economic and social advantage (Foner 2000: 241). Their participation in the transnational social field would further strengthen transnationalism, and would make this case very different from the experiences of earlier immigrants in the United States. An exciting and important area for more research is the question of whether transnationalism will persist—a question that can only be answered by long-term research among communities such as the Yucatecans in Dallas.

References

Achor, Shirley
1991   *Mexican Americans in a Dallas Barrio*. Tucson: University of Arizona Press.

Adler, Rachel H.
2000   "Human Agency in International Migration: The Maintenance of Transnational Social Fields by Yucatecan Migrants in a Southwestern City." *Estudios Mexicanos/ Mexican Studies* 16:165–187.
2002   "Patron-Client Ties, Ethnic Entrepreneurship and Transnational Migration: The Case of Yucatecans in Dallas, Texas." *Urban Anthropology and Studies of Cultural Systems and World Economic Development* 31:129–162.

Ainslie, Ricardo
1998   "Cultural Mourning, Immigration, and Engagement: Vignettes from the Mexican Experience." In *Crossings: Mexican Immigration in Interdisciplinary Perspectives*. M. M. Suárez-Orozco, ed. Pp. 285–300. Cambridge: Harvard University Press.

Alvarez, Robert R.
1991   *Familia: Migration and Adaptation in Baja and Alta California 1800–1975*. Berkeley: University of California Press.

Appadurai, Arjun
1991   "Global Ethnoscapes." In *Recapturing Anthropology*. R. Fox, ed. Pp. 191–210. Santa Fe: School of American Research Press.
1996a   "Sovereignty without Territoriality: Notes for a Postnational Geography." In *The Geography of Identity*. P. Yaeger, ed. Pp. 40–58. Ann Arbor: University of Michigan Press.
1996b   *Modernity at Large: Cultural Dimensions of Globalization*. Minneapolis: University of Minnesota Press

Barth, Frederik, ed.
1969   *Ethnic Groups and Boundaries: The Social Organization of Cultural Difference.* London: George Allen and Unwin.

Basch, Linda, Nina Glick-Schiller, and Cristina Szanton-Blanc
1994   *Nations Unbound: Transnational Projects, Postcolonial Predicaments, and Deterritorialized Nation-States.* New York: Gordon and Breach.

Beil, Laura
1995   "Parkland Wants Price's Protests Restricted." In *Dallas Morning News,* March 8.

Bever, Sandra Weinstein
1999   "Migration, Household Economy, and Gender: A Comparative Study of Households in a Rural Yucatec Migrant Community," unpublished Ph.D. dissertation, Southern Methodist University.

Bonfil Batalla, Guillermo
1996   *México Profundo: Reclaiming a Civilization.* Philip A. Dennis, translator. Austin: University of Texas Press.

Brannon, Jeffery and Eric N. Baklanoff
1987   *Agrarian Reform and Public Enterprise in Mexico: The Political Economy of Yucatan's Henequen Industry.* Tuscaloosa: University of Alabama Press.

Brettell, Caroline
1979   "Emigrar Para Voltar: A Portuguese Ideology of Return Migration." In *Papers in Anthropology* 20:1–20.
1982   *We Have Already Cried Many Tears: The Stories of Three Portuguese Migrant Women.* Cambridge, MA: Schenkman Press.
2000   "Theorizing Migration in Anthropology: The Social Construction of Networks, Identities, Communities and Globalscapes." In *Migration Theory: Talking Across Disciplines.* Caroline B. Brettell and James F. Hollifield, eds. Pp. 97–135. New York: Routledge.

Brettell, Caroline, Dennis Cordell, and James Hollifield
1996   "The New Dallas: Immigrants, Ethnic Entrepreneurship and Cultural Diversity. Dallas: Southern Methodist University," unpublished grant proposal.

Burns, Allan
1993   *Maya in Exile: Guatemalans in Florida.* Philadelphia: Temple University Press.

Cardoso, Lawrence A.
1980   *Mexican Emigration to the United States 1897–1931: Socioeconomic Patterns.* Tucson: University of Arizona Press.

Carmack, Robert M., Janine Gasco, and Gary H. Gossen
1996   *The Legacy of Mesoamerica: History and Culture of a Native Civilization.* Upper Saddle River, NJ: Prentice Hall.

Castañeda, Quetzil E.
1996   *In the Museum of Maya Culture.* Minneapolis: University of Minnesota Press.

Chávez, Leo R.
1998   *Shadowed Lives: Undocumented Immigrants in American Society.* Fort Worth: Harcourt Brace Jovanovich.

Cheng, Shu-Ju Ada
1999   "Labor Migration and International Sexual Division of Labor: A Feminist Perspective." In *Gender and Immigration.* G. Kelson and D. DeLaet, eds. Pp. 38–58. New York: New York University Press.

Conord, Bruce and June Conord
1998   *Adventure Guide to Yucatán: Including Cáncun and Cozumel.* Edison, NJ: Hunter.

Corchado, Alfredo and Frank Trejo
1999   "Urban Renewal: Dallas' Mexican Population Brings Boom Times to Once-Dying Areas, Creates Challenges." In *Dallas Morning News,* September 9.

Dallas Chamber of Commerce
1996   *Dallas at a Glance 1995–96.* Dallas: Dallas Chamber of Commerce.
1999   *Dallas at a Glance 1998–99.* Dallas: Dallas Chamber of Commerce.
2000   *International Dallas 2000–2001.* Dallas: Dallas Chamber of Commerce.

Dinerman, Ina R.
1982   *Migrants and Stay and Homes: A Comparative Study of Rural Migration from Michoacán, Mexico.* Monograph Number 5. San Diego: University of California Center for U.S.-Mexican Studies.

Dulaney, W. Marvin
1993   "Whatever Happened to the Civil Rights Movement in Dallas, Texas?" In *Essays on the American Civil Rights Movement.* W. Dulaney and K. Underwood, eds. Pp. 66–95. Arlington: The University of Texas at Arlington by Texas A&M University Press.

Dufrense, Lucie and Uli Locher
1995   "The Mayas and Cáncun: Migration Under Conditions of Peripheral Urbanization." *Labour, Capital and Society* 28: 176–202.

Durand, Jorge and Douglas Massey
  1992   "Mexican Migration to the United States: A Critical Re-
          view." *Latin American Research Review* 27:3–42.

Elmendorf, Mary
  1970   *Nine Mayan Women: A Village Faces Change.* NY: Schenkman.

Farriss, Nancy M.
  1984   *Maya Society Under Colonial Rule: The Collective Enterprise
          of Survival.* Princeton: Princeton University Press.

Foner, Nancy
  1978   *Jamaica Farewell: Jamaican Migrants in London.* Berkeley:
          University of California Press.
  1997   "The Immigrant Family: Cultural Legacies and Cultural
          Changes." *International Migration Review* 31:961–974.
  1999   "Anthropology and the Study of Immigration." *American
          Behavioral Scientist* 42:1268–1270.
  2000   *From Ellis Island to JFK: New York's Two Great Waves of Im-
          migration.* New Haven: Yale University Press.

Freidel, David, Linda Schele, and Joy Parker
  1993   *Maya Cosmos: Three Thousand Years on the Shaman's Path.*
          New York: William Morrow.

Friedlander, Judith
  1975   *Being Indian in Hueyapan: A Study of Forced Identity in Con-
          temporary Mexico.* New York: St. Martin's Press.

Georges, Eugenia
  1990   *The Making of a Transnational Community: Migration, Devel-
          opment, and Cultural Change in the Dominican Republic.*
          New York: Columbia University Press.

Giddens, Anthony
  1979   *Central Problems in Social Theory: Action, Structure, and
          Contradiction in Social Analysis.* Berkeley: University of
          California Press.
  1984   *The Constitution of Society: Outline of the Theory of Structur-
          ation.* Cambridge: Polity Press.
  1995   *Politics, Sociology and Social Theory: Encounters with Classical
          and Contemporary Social Thought.* Cambridge: Polity Press.

Glick-Schiller, Nina, Linda Basch, and Cristina Szanton-Blanc
  1995   "From Immigrant to Transmigrant: Theorizing Transna-
          tional Migration." *Anthropological Quarterly* 68:48–63.

Goldring, Luin
  1996   "Gendered Memory: Constructions of Rurality among
          Mexican Transnational Migrants." In *Creating the Country-*

side: The Politics of Rural and Environmental Discourse. E. M. Dupuis and P. Vandergeest, eds. Pp. 301–329. Philadelphia: Temple University Press.

1999 "The Power of Status in Transnational Social Fields." In *Transnationalism from Below.* M. Smith and L. Guarnizo, eds. Pp. 165–195. New Brunswick: Transaction.

Grasmuck, Sherri and Patricia R. Pessar
1991 *Between Two Islands: Dominican International Migration.* Berkeley: University of California Press.

Grimes, Kimberly M.
1998 *Crossing Borders: Changing Social Identities in Southern Mexico.* Tucson: The University of Arizona Press.

Guarnizo, Luis Eduardo, Michael Peter Smith
1999 "The Locations of Transnationalism." In *Transnationalism From Below.* M. Smith and L. Guarnizo, eds. Pp. 3–34. New Brunswick: Transaction.

Guendelman, S. and A. Perez-Itriago.
1987 "Double Lives: The Changing Role of Women in Seasonal Migration." *Women's Studies* 13:249–271.

Gutiérrez, David G.
1998 "Ethnic Mexicans and the Transformation of 'American' Social Space: Reflections on Recent History." In *Crossings: Mexican Immigration in Interdisciplinary Perspectives.* M. M. Suárez-Orozco, ed. Pp. 307–335. Cambridge: Harvard University Press.

Haenn, Nora
n.d. "Images of the Other in Tourism: Yucatán as a Case Example," unpublished manuscript.

Hagan, Jacqueline Maria
1994 *Deciding to be Legal: A Maya Community in Houston.* Philadelphia: Temple University Press.
1998 "Social Networks, Gender and Immigrant Incorporation: Resources and Constraints." *American Sociological Review* 63:55–67.

Hannerz, Ulf
1996 *Transnational Connections: Culture, People, Places.* New York: Routledge.

Hervik, Peter
1999 *Mayan People within and Beyond Boundaries: Social Categories and Lived Identity in Yucatán.* Amsterdam: Harwood Academic Publishers.

Ho, Christine
1999   "Caribbean Transnationalism as a Gendered Process."
        Latin American Perspectives 25:34–54.

Hondagneu-Sotelo, Pierrette
1994   *Gendered Transitions: Mexican Experiences of Immigration.*
        Berkeley: University of California Press.

Instituto Nacional de Estadistica, Geographía e Informática (INEGI)
1996   *Yucatán: Resultados Definitivos Tabulados Basicos.* Aguascal-
        ientes, Mexico: Instituto Nacionál de Estadística
        Geografía e Informática.

Joseph, Gilbert M.
1982   *Revolution from Without: Yucatán, Mexico and the United
        States 1880–1924.* New York: Cambridge University Press.

Kearney, Michael
1991   "Borders and Boundaries of State and Self at the End of
        Empire." *Journal of Historical Sociology* 4:52–74.
1995   "The Local and the Global: The Anthropology of Global-
        ization and Transnationalism. "*Annual Review of Anthro-
        pology* 24:547–565.
2000   "Transnational Oaxacan Indigenous Identity: The Case of
        Mixtecs and Zapotecs." *Identities* 7:173–195.

Kibria, Nazli
1993   *Family Tightrope: The Changing Lives of Vietnamese Ameri-
        cans.* Princeton: Princeton University Press.

Kintz, Ellen
1990   *Life Under the Tropical Canopy.* Chicago: Holt, Rinehart and
        Winston.

Koltyk, Jo Ann
1998   *New Pioneers in the Heartland: Hmong Life in Wisconsin.*
        Boston: Allyn and Bacon.

Labrecque, Maria France
1998   "Women and Gendered Production in Rural Yucatán:
        Some Local Features of Globalization." *Urban Anthropology*
        27:233–262.

Levitt, Peggy
2001   *The Transnational Villagers.* Berkeley: University of Califor-
        nia Press.

Light, Ivan and Edna Bonacich
1988   *Immigrant Entrepreneurs: Koreans in Los Angeles, 1965–1982.*
        Berkeley: University of CA Press.

Lomnitz, Larissa and Marisol Perez-Lizaur
1987   *A Mexican Elite Family, 1820–1980: Kinship, Class and Culture*. Princeton: Princeton University Press.

Lopez, Nora and Todd J. Gillman
1997   "Kirk Advocates DISD Crackdown against Protesters." In *The Dallas Morning News*, February 13.

Loucky, James
1992   "Central American Refugees: Learning New Skills in the USA." In *Anthropology: Understanding Human Adaptation*. H. Howard, ed. New York: Harper Collins.

Mahler, Sarah J.
1995   *American Dreaming: Immigrant Life on the Margins*. Princeton: Princeton University Press.
1999   "Theoretical and Empirical Contributions Toward a Research Agenda for Transnationalism." In *Transnationalism From Below*. M. Smith and L. Guarnizo, eds. Pp. 64–100. New Brunswick: Transaction.

Margolis, Maxine
1998   *An Invisible Minority: Brazilians in New York City*. Boston: Allyn and Bacon.

Massey, Douglas S., Rafael Alarcón, Jorge Durand, and Humberto Gonzalez
1987   *Return to Aztlan: The Social Process of International Migration from Western Mexico*. Berkeley: University of California Press.

Massey, Douglas S., Joaquin Arango, Graeme Hugo, Ali Kouaouci, Adela Pellegrino, and J. Edward Taylor
1993   "Theories of International Migration: A Review and Appraisal." *Population and Development Review* 20: 431–66.

Massey, Douglas S., Luin Goldring, and Jorge Durand
1994   "Continuities in Transnational Migration: An Analysis of Nineteen Mexican Communities." *American Journal of Sociology* 99:1492–1533.

Menjívar, Cecilia
1999   "The Intersection of Work and Gender." *American Behavioral Scientist* 42:601–627.

Min, Pyong Gap
1998   *Changes and Conflicts: Korean Immigrant Families in New York*. Boston: Allyn and Bacon.

Mines, Richard and Ricardo Anzaldua
  1982   *New Migrants vs. Old Migrants: Alternative Labor Market Structures in the California Citrus Industry.* Monograph Number 9. San Diego: University of California Center for U.S.-Mexican Studies.

Nagengast, Carole and Michael Kearney
  1990   "Mixtec Ethnicity: Social Identity, Political Consciousness, and Political Activism." *Latin American Research Review* 25:61–91.

Nagengast, Carole, Rodolfo Stavenhagen, and Michael Kearney
  1992   *Human Rights and Indigenous Workers: The Mixtecs of Mexico and the United States.* San Diego: Center for U.S.-Mexican Studies, University of California.

Payne, Darwin
  1994   *Big D:Triumphs and Troubles of an American Supercity in the 20th Century.* Dallas: Three Forks Press.

Pérez, Lisandro
  1986   "Immigrant Economic Adjustment and Family Organization: The Cuban Success Story Reexamined." *International Migration Review* 20:4–20.

Pessar, Patricia R.
  1995a   "On the Homefront and in the Workplace: Integrating Immigrant Women into Feminist Discourse." *Anthropological Quarterly* 68: 37–47.
  1995b   *A Visa For a Dream: Dominicans in the United States.* Boston: Allyn and Bacon.

Portes, Alejandro
  1995   "Children of Immigrants: Segmented Assimilation and its Determinants." In *The Economic Sociology of Immigration: Essays on Networks, Ethnicity and Entrepreneurship.* A. Portes, ed. Pp. 248–279. New York: Russell Sage Foundation.

Portes, Alejandro and Min Zhou
  1993   "The New Second Generation: Segmented Assimilation and its Variants." *Annals of the American Academy of Political and Social Sciences* 530:74–96.

Press, Irwin
  1975   *Tradition and Adaptation.* Westport: Greenwood Press.

Re Cruz, Alicia
  1996   *The Two Milpas of Chan Kom: Scenarios of a Maya Village Life.* Albany: State University of New York Press.

Redfield, Robert
1941 *The Folk Culture of Yucatán*. Chicago: University of Chicago Press.

Repak, Terry A.
1995 *Waiting on Washington: Central American Workers in the Nation's Capital*. Philadelphia: Temple University Press.

Restall, Matthew
1997 *The Maya World: Yucatec Culture and Society 1550–1850*. Stanford: Stanford University Press.

Rivera Salgado, Gaspar
1999 "Mixtec Activism in Oaxacalifornia: Transborder Grassroots Political Strategies." *American Behavioral Scientist* 42: 1439–1458.

Rodríguez, Nestor
1996 "The Battle for the Border: Notes on Autonomous Migration, Transnational Communities, and the State." *Social Justice* 23:21–37.

Rouse, Roger
1989 "Mexican Migration to the United States: Family Relations in the Development of a Transnational Migrant Circuit," unpublished Ph.D. dissertation, Stanford University.
1991 "Mexican Migration and the Social Space of Postmodernism." *Diaspora* 1:8–23.

Sassen, Saskia
1991 *The Global City: New York, London, Tokyo*. Princeton: Princeton University Press.
1995 "Immigration and Local Labor Markets." In *The Economic Sociology of Immigration: Essays on Networks, Ethnicity, and Entrepreneurship*. A. Portes, ed. Pp. 87–127. New York: Russell Sage Foundation.
2000 *Cities in a World Economy*. Thousand Oaks, California: Pine Forge Press.

Scott, James C.
1985 *Weapons of the Weak: Everyday Forms of Peasant Resistance*. New Haven: Yale University Press.

Smith, Michael Peter and Luis Eduardo Guarnizo
1999a "The Locations of Transnationalism." In *Transnationalism from Below*. M. Smith and L. Guarnizo, eds. Pp. 3–34. New Brunswick: Transaction.

Smith, Robert C.
1993   "Los Ausente Siempre Presentes: The Imagining, Making and Politics of a Transnational Community between New York City and Ticuani, Puebla." New York: Institute of Latin American and Iberian Studies, Columbia University.
1999   "Transnational Localities: Community, Technology and the Politics of Membership within the Context of Mexico and U.S. Migration." In *Transnationalism from Below*. M. Smith and L. Guarnizo, eds. Pp. 196–238. New Brunswick: Transaction.

Warman, Arturo
1980   *We Come to Object: The Peasants of Morelos and the National State.* Baltimore: Johns Hopkins Press.

Wells, Allen
1985   *Yucatan's Gilded Age: Haciendas, Henequen, and International Harvester, 1860–1915.* Albuquerque: University of New Mexico Press.

West, Robert C.
1964   "The Natural Regions of Middle America." In *Handbook of Middle American Indians, vol. 1.* Robert C. West, ed. Pp. 363–383. Austin: University of Texas Press.

Wilson, Tamar Diana
1993   "Theoretical Approaches to Mexican Wage Migration." *Latin American Perspectives* 20:98–129.

Index